Face the Phase

A Christian Woman's Guide to Aspects of Life

Patricia Schmidgall

ISBN 979-8-88851-767-3 (Paperback)
ISBN979-8-88851-768-0 (Digital)

Covenant Books
11661 Hwy 707
Murrells Inlet, SC 29576
www.covenantbooks.com

Contents

Preface

Every woman goes through multiple phases as she progresses through life. I have been motivated to write about these phases because I believe that we, as women, need to spend some time dissecting life to live it to the fullest. Life is a slippery slope that propels one forward at a breakneck speed. How can we mentally put on the brakes? I believe that it is a matter of visualization. We must decompartmentalize living into states of experience. As it is spread out for study, life becomes less menacing and more prone to control. Predetermine life goals and align your phases in a synchronizing manner. To do this, it is imperative to determine your value system, your roles, your plans to resolve conflict, and your methods to cope with failure. We are not helpless victims of circumstance, but rather active participants in every phase of life. Vital to success is the ability to operate with humility, maintain a modicum of flexibility, and establish and retain clear objectives. In this book, the names, experiences, and examples have been altered to preserve confidentiality. However, the universality of the need to deal with what life thrusts upon us is made apparent.

Phases require psychological adjustment, as a myriad of emotions are involved. How can one be successful with a massive subdivision of self? The answer is very simple. *Slow down.* Be aware of where you are in life and where you are headed. Use quiet time each day to ask God for guidance. Embrace God's plan for your life as well as your own abilities. Periodically review your game plan and allow everything to fall into place.

Since God is no respecter of persons, cling to the scripture Psalm 37:23, which reads, "If the Lord delights in a man's way, He makes his steps firm; though he stumble he will not fall, for the Lord upholds him with His hand." Psalm 37:25 says, "I was young and now I am old, yet I have never seen the righteous forsaken or their children begging bread."

Life's phases will not always turn out according to plan even when carefully designed. Just remember, what may appear as a failure to you is part of God's sovereign plan. If we ask Him to be our guide, it will work out in the end.

Simplify life by breaking it into phases, then live, love, and enjoy. You only go around once. It's your phase. Relax. Be strong.

Romance

Wine and Honey

For I peered into the future, far as mind could grasp.
Saw a picture of my love and knew that it would last.

Saw my universe immersed in waves of azure hue.
As the heavens rained down kindness, gentle as the dew.

Heard a whisper in the treetops like a soft, warm breeze
A song of comfort so serene it lulled me with ease.

Felt his caress upon my arm, a soft, gentle touch
And I knew my heart was lost to one I loved so much.

A hint of wine and honey was the taste upon his lips.
Sweet reminder of a flower with nectar that drips.

The fragrance on his pillow that lingers in the air,
Wafts round and beckons me to follow without care.

From the present to the future, I'm wholly entranced,
Wrapped in romance so divine, I know it can't be chance.

*****

Amber contemplated marriage almost daily. The thought had wrapped itself around her mind and greeted her every morning. Sometimes it prodded her awake at night with a little squeeze. Actually, the thing that had her in its clutches didn't have a death grip. It was more like a passionate hug.

Don't misunderstand. Amber was not disconcerted, nor could she disparage her single life. Her heart had beaten to an ordinary existence—a loving family, a house in a small town, a good education, and a normal middle-class upbringing. But just when she had developed a modicum of certainty about her life, there was a tremor that rattled her foundation. It started as a shiver of underlying discontent similar to that which develops in the contemplations of most womankind at one time or another. Subtly, the inner irritation rose in intensity until, like a mosquito that lands in the middle of your back, it became a force that demanded her full attention.

The quake, which so rudely disrupted her ordinary life, had at its epicenter a six-foot specimen of a man. You guessed it. She was in love. For twenty-one years, she formulated an opinion about Mr. Right. He needed to be stable with a spiritual commitment, and his interests in life needed to be similar to hers. Amber put some traits high on her priority list and hoped that he would be devoted, trustworthy, caring, considerate, hardworking, mature, and reliable. Oh yes, she also dared to hope that he would be tall and handsome.

Amber had to admit that when she met Mr. Right, it felt a little bit like her heart had stopped. Actually, it was probably her breathing that had stopped. At any rate, be it luck, good fortune, perfect timing, or God's will, she hoped that this one would not get away. He did not. Her love grew to be their love and eventually led to "I do."

Romance

The innovation of romance must be the ultimate creation of imagination. This ageless sport requires courage, flexibility, and devotion. Rather than beating your opponent to the finish line, its strategy involves the development of a seamless connection with a partner. Being motivated by a passion rather than by competition is almost counterintuitive. Perhaps that is what makes the game unique. Imagination allows us to escape our competitive nature in order that we can make a dream come true.

The beauty and mystery of romance revolve around a selfless spirit. Egocentrism destroys any chance for victory since synchronization is a crucial element of success. In other words, remember the adage, "In honor preferring one another." This sentience in no way indicates a compulsion to allow someone to walk on you for the sake of becoming a "couple." Rather, it represents the ability to allow another person to complete you as together you help one another accomplish desired goals and aspirations.

Another element of romance is respect. As a relationship becomes more serious, there is a mutual standard of involvement, which must be met by both partners. Life is more than giving and getting or mutual admiration. Ultimately, respect comes into play as temptations and relationship choices are made. Granted, relationships are dynamic in nature, but beyond this flexibility is a solid core of connection, which must not be breached.

Determination also has to play a role in romance. Every relationship has an ebb and flow. How badly do you want a friendship to blossom? Without compromising standards, one should work to preserve what is valuable and discard that which is not viable. Anything worthwhile takes effort. In a relationship, this effort must come from both parties.

Romance means different things to different people. For most, however, it boils down to passion, pleasure, and joy. You find beauty in being together. You enthusiastically anticipate hearing each other's voice. Absence from one another is equivalent to sensory deprivation.

A romantic relationship causes you to put your best foot forward. The goal is to open the eyes of your partner to the fact that without you, he will be losing the most awesome thing that life has to offer. How many hours of primping do you believe goes into this endeavor? The whole purpose of romance is to commit to something bigger than oneself and to ultimately develop a wonderful life together.

For some, romance and the exciting process of wooing someone is the totality of their goal. As such, their friendships are short-lived affairs. Once the excitement is over, they are ready to move on. For these people, romance is the nectar that they use to attract a bee. Once the bee is snared, the romance ceases. For them, familiarity breeds contempt.

It takes creativity and hard work to maintain a romance through the stages of dating, engagement, and finally marriage. The following are some thoughts pertaining to attaining longevity of romance.

1. *Tenderness:* Show kindness and compassion. Say "I'm sorry" as often as is necessary and "I love you" with frequency. Be prepared to protect and appreciate your partner as you value his interests.

2. *Dedication:* Being faithful to your mate is probably number one on the priority list. Trust and commitment are built upon the foundation of faithfulness. Beyond this, however, it is crucial to respect your partner and to patiently tend to his needs, be they emotional, physical, or sexual. Dedication gives a relationship true purpose.

3. *Communication:* This involves both speaking and listening through mutual exchange. It is important to be open and honest at all times with your partner. Be an active listener especially in times of conflict. Remember that secrets kill romance.

4. *Balance:* Do not always demand your way. There should be reciprocal giving and taking as well as ongoing negotiation. This means that you should take a genuine interest in your mate's desires. Compromise is the key component of balance.

5. *Dominance:* Power struggles will destroy romance. In this sphere is anger, withdrawal, and insensitivity to the other person. This will definitely quash romance. Our goal should be to maintain a healthy friendship.

Biblical Perspective

God is the author of romance. He created woman and brought her to man as a suitable mate. This is recorded in Genesis 2:22. The intimacy between a couple is vital enough that a magnificent love poem is recorded in chapter 1, verses 2 to 4 of the Song of Solomon. The woman says, "Let him kiss me with the kisses of his mouth—for your love is more delightful than wine." The man responds, "Pleasing is the fragrance of your perfumes; your name is like perfume poured out." They proceed to correspond lovingly to one another with passionate comparisons—a sachet of myrrh resting between my breasts, a cluster of henna blossoms, eyes like doves, a rose of Sharon, a lily of the valley, an apple tree among the trees of the forest, and the like. In all, there are eight chapters devoted to the love between two young people.

The innovation of romance began with the creation of woman as a companion for man. The beauty of this aspect of life is that it creates excitement and mystique in a relationship and is the element that adds spice to a marriage. The journey from friendship to love is designed by God to last until "death do us part." Our goal must be to absorb the attributes associated with romance and allow them to be our guide to a healthy and happy relationship.

Why do you think that a perfect romantic relationship is represented in the Bible? I believe that it is because God refers to the church or believers as His bride. Christ wants to make the ideal companionship obvious in order that we can understand how He wants to relate to us. The perfect romance, then, is not purely sexual in nature. Rather, it is much deeper. God refers to Himself as a jealous God. He wants His bride all to Himself, not to be shared with the world and its cares. God wants us to spend time with Him through prayer and study of His Word. His love for us is the ultimate example of selflessness in that He gave His own life for us. The relationship is designed to be reciprocal as the walk together is filled with joy.

Childhood

Pigtails and Banana Peels

Why's that banana peel under the chair?
Didn't I just sweep and clean under there?
So much for spotless, I'm not in despair.
The culprit has pigtails and light brown hair

Her castle's a table with a big sheet.
From underneath I see two little feet.
The old dog's her dragon, but he's asleep.
She'll wake him with hugs and a special treat.

I know I heard a splash and then a swish.
Oh, please tell me she's not feeding the fish.
Is that a corn curl floating in his dish?
Mr. Fins seems to be smiling in bliss.

A pair of pink socks but only one shoe.
I'm sure she came into the house with two.
Let me think, where did we go? What did we do?
I'll have to give up. I have not a clue.

I made some cookies we could decorate,
But none were for some future date.
There was no way that she and I could wait.
I must admit we ate and ate.

Children were fun, grandchildren much better.
I don't have to do things by the letter.

Have joys no end and age no tether,
The fun times we have could last forever.

*****

It had been a long day, and I was exhausted. As I sat down at the table to relax with a book and a cup of tea, I found myself face-to-face with the most incredible bouquet of flowers that I have ever seen. My grandchildren had picked them with me during a walk that day. The arrangement was not incredible because of its beauty, but rather for the fun memory that it evoked. The vase was a clear glass serving bowl filled with water. Floating on the top were the heads of about twenty dandelions as well as the blooms from several varieties of flowers from Grandpa's garden. The children pick only the pretty parts of the flowers. So…we floated the flower heads in the glass bowl. Just for fun we added a couple of floating candles. We then carried the pretty arrangement to the only room in our house without a window—a bathroom. I lit the candles, turned off the lights, and let the beautiful creation light up the room; then we all oohed and aahed. It's a fun routine that's repeated frequently with a multiplicity of variety. Sometimes we add food coloring to the water, sometimes we find pretty rocks for the bottom of the bowl, and once we even let Mr. Fins swim around under the flowers. The only thing that does not vary is the length of flower stems or, shall we say, lack of length, for, you know, it's important to only pick the pretty part of a flower.

Childhood

God's most awesome creation has to be children. No thrill compares to holding your own child or grandchild in your arms. Each child has potential to elevate society and redirect the fate of the world. But when they're in your arms, you're not thinking about the world. You're just overwhelmed by love for the child and a need to shield them from any bad thing that could ever come their way. When they are small, it seems as though time is dragging, you are dragging, and everything is moving in slow motion except for the children with their boundless energy. It is only in retrospect that memories of the good times suppress ongoing exhaustion.

Soon, like a vapor, the days of infancy blend into the toddler stage of life. During this period of development, children know things by tasting, seeing, hearing, touching, and doing. Anything with reach is fair game. Before long, however, the days of chasing a little human vacuum cleaner around change into hours of playing pretend.

Behind our house is a big oak tree with a twenty-foot rope swing hanging from one of its branches. As I was pushing our grandson, he kept yelling "higher, higher!" I retorted, "I can't because you might fall off, and I would be obliged to dive on the ground to give you a soft landing." At first, he looked incredulous. Then, realizing it was an opportunity for some make-believe, we were off and running.

"What would happen then, Grandma?"

"You would have to call the rescue squad because I would be as flat as a pancake!"

"Let's try it" was his automatic response." Yeah…right! Children love to use their imaginations and are game for almost anything.

Representational thought has developed from those first couple of years of hands-on experience. New skills built on past experiences allow for interplay between the child and other children or the child and adults. Granted, memory strategies are limited, but with a little interaction, it is surprising just how much information is stored in those little heads. To demonstrate this fact, I will describe a game that I used to play with my children when they were preschool age. Together we would pore over magazines and rip out pictures of flowers, animals, rocks, and interesting items. We would then glue these on a piece of paper in sets of three. When we were finished, I would point to a set of pictures and ask questions that stimulated memory. Which of these items feels hard? Which picture smells the best? Which of these pictures shows something that could love you? The answers were designed to be obvious, but without memory, the game would be impossible. It was interesting to note that, at times, the child would touch or smell the pictures before answering. It is so fun to share games, social fantasy, and activities with our children and grandchildren. It's not difficult to be warm and responsive to their antics because they really are cute. Oh, sometimes they can be frustrating, but they have a way of winning your heart.

What are some aspects of relationships that are vital during those young years? First of all, children crave constant love. Every child needs to know that they can never be so naughty that they are not loved. Follow every consequence to correct negative behavior with hugs and praise for good things about the child.

Also, consistency is vital. We all need to know what is expected from us. There is comfort and security found in an orderly existence. From a comfort zone, children gain confidence to explore the world around them and to try new things.

A critical aspect of child rearing involves instilling self-confidence. To my chagrin, I am aware of one father who continually berated his son by finding fault in everything he did. This boy was constantly told that he would never amount to anything. It was not until his adult years that this boy began finding himself. Even now he has lapses of courage related to his struggle to believe that he is a capable adult.

Organization is another key aspect of childhood. LEGO bricks were one of my children's favorite toys. We bought containers with a lot of drawers to separate the LEGO bricks into various sizes and shapes. The children's job was to put the LEGO bricks into the correct drawer when they were finished building their creations. The reasoning behind this chore was to allow them to more easily build their next project. The flaw in this thinking was that the boys never wanted to tear apart anything that they built. I think the organizational plan transformed into building little shelves to display the awesome creations until they fell apart. Unfortunately, this propensity for organization did not translate into keeping a neat room. It was reserved for LEGO sets, puzzles, games, and important things; perhaps with time...? Children thrive on routine, organization, and a constant environment. They learn to expect age-appropriate restrictions and consequences. Structure leads to a sense of order and provides a stable base from which to thrive and develop.

Parents must slowly adjust their intervention in respect to the child's maturing skills. It is important to let them try things even if they fail. Praise success and support their effort when they fail. At a young age, children acquire thoughts and feelings about themselves. This evaluation of self or self-esteem will follow them throughout life. Recently, I stifled a gasp as my three-year-old grandson knocked a glass of red juice off the table and onto the beige carpet before I could get a lid on his cup. He smiled and patted my hand and said, "Don't worry, Grandma. It was just an accident." In that moment, it was obvious that he had been raised with kindness. There was no fear in his demeanor or voice. He simply wanted to assure me that everything was okay even if it looked like a mess. And...do you know... he was right.

It is not long before the innocent young years blend into middle childhood. My first grader came home from school with an important announcement. "If you pick your nose in school, you have to go wash your hands." My obvious question was, "Have you ever had to go wash your hands?" He assured me that he had not, but I had to resist the urge to rush to school to assure the teacher that not every behavior that a child exhibits has been learned at home.

By middle childhood, the total amount of knowledge held in long-term storage has developed into an extensive memory. Based on these memories, children are able to make inferences so that not only can they remember, but they can also predict. If I eat all those gross vegetables on my plate, I can get a yummy dessert. If I make my bed all week, I can earn a reward.

They also begin to gain knowledge through cooperative and competitive peer interaction. As the concept of teamwork develops, the task of working with a team to achieve a goal seems painfully tedious. Who wants to throw the basketball to a teammate? Isn't it more fun to try to make the basket by yourself? Eventually, the merits of working with others to achieve a goal begins to make sense and is actually fun.

Children in middle childhood have the ability to describe how they feel, what they believe, and how they want to be perceived by others. A social self develops as children form meaningful relationships with friends. Social comparisons occur as well as a sense of identity. It is vital that parents are supportive of children at this age and provide them with security.

By the age of ten or eleven, recreational time spent with peers usually surpasses time spent with family. The lessons on sharing, equity, and fairness accompany expanded socialization. Rules in respect to appropriate interpersonal behaviors are within their grasp. Bullying, suitable conversations, and behaviors must be stressed. Close monitoring of electronic media is crucial.

At home, parents give children in middle childhood more responsibility and deal with them through reasoning. *Chores!* I still remember my tasks...clean your room and make your bed. It is amazing how many things can be hidden under the pillows and bedspread to give a room a neat appearance. My parents reasoned that I was old enough to do a little housework, and I reasoned that what they didn't see couldn't hurt them. The memory fades as to when this habit became extinct, but I assure you that there is nothing hidden under my bedspread now. Basically, it is good to keep the chores simple and age-appropriate: feed the dog, put your dirty socks in the hamper, hang your coat on the hook, and so forth. Usually, a little monitoring is required, but for the most part, the children enjoy taking ownership of their assigned tasks, especially if the chores are tied to a reward.

From infancy through middle childhood, a child matures and develops at a rate unparalleled to any other time in life. With increased cognition comes enhanced emotional development, self-esteem, and the ability to predict and make inferences. There is also an understanding of right from wrong. Moral and spiritual instruction and modeling are vital. As small children, we always went to Sunday school and had devotions at home as a family. These lessons carried me through the next complicated years.

In retrospect, I value all the life lessons taught and modeled by my parents. Hopefully, each of us can gently guide our children into maturity and help them become the God-designed person they were meant to be.

Biblical Perspective

Not long ago, I watched a young mother interact with her infant. She would hold her up and tell her how beautiful she was. Tiny babies look wherever their eyes happen to look, so she would move the baby around until their eyes met. From this vantage point, she would then repeat her message of love in between a kiss or two on the cheek. This must be how God feels toward us. First John 4:19 says, "We love God because He first loved us." Unfortunately, this love isn't absorbed through osmosis. It must be explained. However, it is quite difficult to describe a love so pure and all-encompassing. In Matthew 18:10, we find that before we even knew God or knew about Him, He assigned us each an angel that is before His throne interceding on our behalf. We are God's priority. He loves us.

Children were a priority for Jesus. He told the disciples to bring the children to Him so that He could bless them, as recorded in Matthew 15:14. Children are a heritage from the Lord according to Psalm 127:3–5. As such, it is our responsibility to teach them about God's love. In Proverbs 22:6, parents are admonished to train up a child in the way he should go so that when he is old, he will not depart from what is right. Training is a crucial part of parenting.

If we as parents do our job, it will be automatic for our children to lean on God's Word, to talk to Him, and to believe in His promises. It will not occur to them to try to slide into heaven by some alternate route. They will know the path of righteousness. Does this mean they will never stray? Of course, this is not the case. It just means that they have a solid footing on which to walk.

In addition to teaching children about God's love and training them to follow a righteous path, adults should help them understand that religion is active rather than passive. First, they must accept Jesus as their Savior and then be taught to practice the Christian walk. If we tell children that it makes Jesus happy when they tell the truth, share, or are kind to others, they slowly internalize these principles. Before long, it is within their grasp to relate to God through behavior. Very early on, I realized that if God was happy with my good behavior, then He must be sad when I am naughty. That knowledge did not always translate into good behavior. Just ask my little brother. I convinced him that a monster lived in the basement of our home. Then I hid under the basement steps and growled at him when he went downstairs. If I remember correctly, this was when I learned a painful lesson about repentance. Sunday school, family Bible time, and daily interaction with godly parents provided ample instruction about God's love and His expectations. Over time, I grew to understand and internalize right from wrong and good from bad.

So childhood presents us as adults with the challenges of relaying the message of God's love, training Christlike living, and demonstrating that religion is active rather than passive. Our ultimate task is to model a life worthy of being patterned after and repeated by those with whom we are responsible. The enormity of the labor is daunting, but the reward can have eternal value.

Adolescence

The Cadence

There's a drum beat in my soul
With a cadence that's so bold
I can't ignore its message
Or deny its bidding call.

As minutes of life unfurl
Chains that bind I hurl
To reject my comfort zone
And explore a pathless world.

Hear the roar of raging seas,
Crashing breakers that don't cease
Or solitude of forests
With their feathered symphonies.

Crystal lakes and fields of grain,
Waterfalls and pounding rain,
Soaring heights and cavern depths,
And any sights that still remain.

My insatiable curse
Is this unquenchable thirst
To see flights as yet unseen
And explore God's universe

*****

A few weeks after the first hint of acne popped out on her face, one of Rachel's best friends called her on the phone with some disturbing news. Tom was planning to ask her to the next school dance. Frankly, she was shy and did not plan on going to the dance, and besides, Rachel was a head taller than Tom. Before long, she was completely obsessed with rehearsing credible excuses for being unable to attend the dance. During sleepless nights, Rachel conjured up notions of having the flu, being grounded, or faking a broken leg. Finally, the dreaded call came, and in an embarrassing and humiliating moment of weakness, she said, "Yes." Well, the dance came and went without incident, and memories of that first date blur into nothingness. However, it was the beginning of many more dates, which would lend themselves to happy memories.

Adolescence

Over the years, I've had a lot of time to think about those dreadful but wonderful years called adolescence. Oh, there were the wobbly, clumsy steps toward finding out who I really was and who I had the potential to become. But, in reality, at that stage of life, the sky was the limit. It was at this time that personal identity formed, and I began to integrate into a coherent being called "self." Development involved a blending of values, roles, and relationships after a period of active exploration. Finally, a fragile person emerged, who was a blend of the recognizable self, the developing self, and the real self.

A friend told me about a sullen girl in her high school class—a young female who had self-mutilated by cutting superficial grooves in her arms with an ink pen. She then used this same pen to stab shallow holes in the backs of her hands. This teenage girl then sat at her desk with a blank look. Across the room was a teacher with a scowl on her face and arms folded tightly as an indication that this troublemaker deserved the harm she had caused herself. My friend cringed to see the blue ink that threaded through the girl's wounds as a permanent reminder of today's breakdown. There was an obvious angry or despondent emotion that needed to be addressed. Intervention was a necessary ingredient in the girl's search for self-worth. This case is extreme, but emotional strain is a common ingredient of adolescence.

For a child in the adolescent phase of life, there is a change in social interaction with the gradual development of a greater symmetry between the youth and the adults. This sometimes occurs smoothly, but at other times, the power structure is fraught with conflict and stress. Obviously, with the girl and her teacher in the classroom, the transition was not smooth. Was the situation irreparable? Probably not. Bumps and bruises are a normal part of learning to walk.

Knowing what a child can expect to occur during adolescent awakening may alleviate some of the stress. First and foremost is the recognition that everything that he or she has done to this point is about to be reworked. To form an optimal sense of identity, an adolescent must explore various options and determine a comfort zone. Within this zone, the young adult is competent and feels secure enough to explore new tasks and to try a variety of roles.

Suddenly, a child is thrust into a time of rapid and dramatic physical change. Accompanying the change is self-consciousness, psychological awareness, and concern about appearance. For the first time in life, the adolescent worries that her/his nose is too big, eyes the wrong color, or eyebrows too bushy. It is very difficult for aging children to separate reality from concept. As such, their actions may hinge on the perceived reality that they are the focus of everyone's attention. Though this "audience" is a figment of their imagination, to adolescents it is very real and as such has an impact on behavior. An adolescent's self-awareness would be considered egocentric if not for its universality.

Not long ago, I stopped to buy a pretzel while shopping at the mall. I was startled to see a girl in the booth across from me with bright-pink hair tied up in three ponytails. Accompanying this pink beauty queen was a friend with about thirty little braids, each tied with a different color ribbon. Then there was a girl with pretty brown hair adorned by one two-inch blonde streak and one boy with a Mohawk spike about six inches out from his head. These friends were laughing and talking like any group of friends. They were polite to those around them and in no way drew attention to themselves other than their appearance. I'm sure they had a mutual understanding of one another and had a friendship based on their harmless frivolity. However, it certainly was an exclusive group. Not unlike other groups of friends, these shared a type of intimacy. It is important to have friends with whom one can share preferences, beliefs, and shortcomings. Loyalty and faithfulness between friends open a forum for self-disclosure without recrimination. There is a definite connection between personal identity and relationships with others.

In respect to relationships with others, adolescents of today face pressures like never before. It comes in the form of electronic media as this vulnerable group of society has to deal with pressure on their phones, tablets, computers, and so forth. Parents are many times unaware of conversations going on right under their noses. This private avenue into an adolescent's life has triggered depression, anger, and self-recrimination. Suicide rates have dramatically increased with an outgrowth of negative bombardment. Children do not have the maturity or training to deal with a negative onslaught of comments either demeaning them or encouraging them into self-destructive behaviors. Even though adolescents are adept at keeping this part of their social life private, parents must attempt to be proactive. Besides asking questions and setting limits, there must be constant support and assurances of the child's worth.

Does conformity to peers mean that the parents' role has been shifted to the back burner? Not really. Parents and peers affect different aspects of a teen's life. Friends influence superficial behaviors such as attire, speech, and mannerisms. Parents continue to have a big impact by sharing their values and beliefs. With strong parental support, the youth has opportunity to return to the ethical base on which he or she was founded. Autonomy and self-expression are outgrowths of warmth, support, and authoritativeness within the family setting.

Thus, physical change, social consciousness, and greater family symmetry are all changes to be expected during adolescence. It is necessary to accept that there will be disagreements. Learn to initiate compromise. Bidirectional influence can be the most freeing aspect of a parent-teen relationship. With an open line of communication, the forces that pull a maturing child in many directions will be stabilized by a healthy home life. It is imperative to admit that sometimes a teen's perspective on an issue may be more accurate than your own. Life changes at a rapid pace. Teens are better able to keep up with vacillation than we are. Core values are rock solid, but it is good to show flexibility on peripheral issues. Let your teen be a teen and try to enjoy their constantly changing self.

Biblical Perspective

The Bible gives multiple scriptures that we as parents can share with our adolescents to comfort and guide them. What are some ways that a young adult can live an effective Christian lifestyle?

1. If we assume that childhood has passed and that the child has now entered the adolescent phase of life, a great place for a maturing child to start would be with the realization that perfection is an unattainable goal. In Joshua 1:9, the teen is commanded to be strong and of good courage, to not be afraid or dismayed for God is with them wherever they go.
2. Adolescents should come to terms with the fact that growth usually is sporadic and hinges on spurts of life lessons. There will be adjustments in behavior and thinking, which are experience-based. Psalm 119:8 encourages adolescents to cleanse their way by heeding God's word. This means that they must guard their mind, body, and heart even when faced with external or internal negativity.
3. Not everyone who goes to church or has a leadership position at church will model perfect behavior. Even at home, parents are human and prone to error. However, teens do have the right to look for a good role model. We as adults should vow to be ready to assume this role at all times. Guide them to scriptures such as Ecclesiastes 12:1, which says to remember your Creator in the days of your youth.

Also encourage them to read Jeremiah 29:11, which says that the Lord wants to give you a future and a hope.

4. Adolescents know right from wrong in their hearts. Faith is emotional rather than cognitive. Cognition will develop slowly with maturity. Expect mistakes. Proverbs 3:5–6 urges the youth to trust the Lord to guide his path.

5. Adolescents must be taught to take control of their thought life. Parents should frequently have them read Philippians 4:8, which says, "Finally brothers and sisters, whatever is true, whatever is noble, whatever is right, whatever is pure, whatever is lovely, whatever is admirable—if anything is excellent or praiseworthy—think about such things."

Have you ever played with those little odd-shaped pieces that can be pushed around inside of a circle with an ink pen? They make delightful patterns that vacillate with the shape of the inserted piece. This is very much like an adolescent's spiritual life. Within its sphere of influence, life may make some unusual patterns consistent with the situation through which the teen is going. However, if God is kept at the center of focus, time and experience will mold these shapes to become more and more like concentric circles with God in the middle. As adults, our job is to gently nudge the adolescent through guidance and modeling.

Teenage Rebellion

My Errant Child

Long are the days I cry for you
And peer for the face that I knew
But the sun blazing in the sky
Has a hot, death glare in its eye.

The child I covet is now obscure.
Does our broken bond have no cure?
O'er several months the gap has grown
As bit by bit discord was sown

I call your name in sad despair,
With a voice that fades in the air.
Outstretched arms reach for you
In hopes that our relationship you'll renew.

    Yet:

I'm not resigned to losing you
And you'll always find me waiting.

*****

Brett was a lanky fifteen-year-old. Until this year, he had been the "perfect son" and a model student. The onset was subtle and barely perceptible to his parents. Yet on the second report card of the school year, he brought home two failing grades. When his mother questioned him, he yelled, "What's it to you?" From that point onward, Brett spiraled downward. Parents took away his electronic devices.

They tried to restrict privilege, but for the first time in his life, he would not listen. Brett stayed out as late as he wished, was tardy to school, moped around all the time, and conversed by yelling obscenities. Brett's dad was angry, and his mother was devastated. Tension at home mounted as everyone played the blame game. Tonight was the last straw. When Brett came home at three in the morning, he smelled like a brewery and was vomiting uncontrollably. His dad wrestled him into the car and held him down while his mom drove to the emergency room.

Brett's rebellion, similar to that of other teens, could be short-lived or long-term depending on the blend of personalities and circumstances. Most rebellious teens outgrow these acting-out behaviors and turn out to be productive citizens. However, at times, intervention is helpful and warranted.

Teenage Rebellion

Abraham Maslow is attributed as once saying, "If the only tool you have is a hammer, every problem you see will look like a nail." This satirical statement indicates the potential dilemma of labeling difficult teens. I cringe every time I hear parents excuse obnoxious behavior by shrugging their shoulders and saying, "Well, he's a teenager." As parents, our roles should fit the needs of the adolescent. Our system should align with techniques that accomplish our established goals. From the time my children were little, I set lofty goals for them. They included a strong spiritual base, exposure to extracurricular activities, a great education, plenty of play time, and constant, enduring love.

Do we believe that our responsibility is to direct the paths of our offspring? If so, then we must act accordingly. Learning and adjustment should be tied to our thought process. Self-destructive behaviors in adolescents are indicative of a cry for parental action. Don't sit back, watch your child spiral downward, and twiddle your thumbs. Excuses are not acceptable! It is time to maneuver into an active parenting role.

The foremost parental responsibility is expansion. Read about adolescence and discover what motivates other teens. Know what is important to your own child. This requires communication and is crucial to successful parenting. Do not get discouraged because it may require some stretching and bending on your part.

Establish core values that are inflexible, then learn to pick your battles with lesser important issues. Despite individual peculiarities and rebellious outbursts, teens crave a secure base from which to explore the world. As we set a positive environment, the teen can be nudged in directions that will not be deleterious. Be willing to fluctuate with life because it is fluid rather than static. Bumps and bruises can be expected. Do not despair. Your child is worth the effort. Rules, consequences, and consistency are all elements at our disposal. Make good use of them.

The bus ride from the house to school was seven miles long with multiple stops. The route was grueling at best and needless to say, the ride was tedious and boring. One obstinate teen took it upon his shoulders to alleviate the drudgery of the other riders by providing some entertainment. First, he decided to surf with an imaginary skateboard by standing in the middle aisle while the bus was moving. When the driver yelled at him to take a seat, he jumped from seat to seat, giving the other students high fives. The driver yelled a more specific command, "Sit in your own seat and stay there." At this point, the teen returned to his seat, sat down, and put his feet up in the air on top of the seat in front of him. The game was over when the other students stopped laughing, so he took this opportunity to drag a pornographic magazine out of his book bag. Needless to say, he was suspended from the bus. Wow, what a treacherous punishment! Now his parents were forced to transport him. The forty-five-minute bus ride was reduced to ten minutes in the comfort of a car. My solution—electronic media, phone, and friends would be banned during the suspension. Oh yes, did I mention that schoolbooks would be the only acceptable reading material other than the Bible? Too harsh? No way! However, I would follow the punishment with an in-depth conversation with my teen to examine why he felt the need to act foolishly. I would then praise him for completing homework and reading assignments.

As parents, we have at our disposal some options to analyze unacceptable behavior and to intervene to thwart its progression. First, we may choose to examine situational dynamics for certain behaviors. Usually there are easily identifiable triggers. The bus student was involved in the dynamics of a captive audience of peers and one adult with the handicap of being distracted with responsibility. The trigger was the opportunity to behave in a manner consistent with getting laughter.

Secondly, it is important to analyze the connection that we as adults have with the teen in respect to his behaviors. This will vary from incident to incident. The temptation is to verbally demean the teen for behaving inappropriately, followed by some punitive measures. Ultimately, however, the adolescent achieved his goals: peers laughed, adults yelled, he received attention. Our hope is that he will learn from the punitive measures meted out by the parents.

Thirdly, it is critical to note how the teen deals with anxiety, anger, and stress. Anxiety and anger could both be tied to low self-esteem. Teens without self-respect feel maligned and misunderstood. Because they do not have self-confidence, these teens find their interactions to be dissatisfying. As such, they feel the need to attract attention in hopes that peers will think more highly of them. However, the more they react negatively, the more they are perceived as being unmotivated and unacceptable. It becomes a vicious circle.

There are two approaches that we as adults can integrate to deal with problem children. The first is rational and involves control. It incorporates an attempt to restore order. Part of this pattern involves negative consequences for bad behavior. Loss of privileges and other punitive measures are designed to establish the knowledge that behavior is tied to consequence. The second part of this approach is equally as important. It involves praise and reward for behavior that alters in respect to the corrective measures. Hopefully, through punishment and reward the teen will gradually begin to behave more consistently in ways that society views as appropriate.

The other approach is subjective and more empathic. Communication is the key element of this means of molding problem behavior. This method is difficult, for it requires self-control and an even demeanor in the face of defiance. Unfortunately, this approach takes time, requires an open mind, and involves willingness to debate issues. Both approaches must convey the message that a teen's behavior is not tied to personal flaws, but rather to poor choices. As his self-esteem elevates, so will his ability to form and develop positive friendships and behaviors.

So the thrust of parental intervention should be aimed at getting the teen to see that his present difficulties and punishments are related to his behavior rather than to him as a person. Sometimes an adolescent is insecure because of guilt and shame over his inability to function without conflict. Others are simply obstinate and angry because they must comply with demands that they perceive to be unjust and unfair. At any rate, a teen in a state of rebellion will resist change. At times, they will overtly act out, and at other times, they will slyly manipulate. Where the parent sees a facade of compliance, peers get to view the true self. What can our plan of action be when cooperation and motivation are absent?

Following are some considerations in respect to dealing with challenging teens:

1. Do not get involved in the show. Yelling is not an effective way to change behavior, and it invites the teen to yell back. Confrontation should be avoided.
2. Expect some aggressiveness. When a person knows in his heart that what he is doing is wrong, he will sometimes feel the need to support the actions intensely.
3. Accountability should be an expected consequence of words and actions. Tie meaningful punishments to unacceptable behavior Use reward as a consequence for positive change.
4. If you discipline with love instead of anger, it will help you calm yourself down and behave rationally.
5. Do not frustrate the situation by giving long lectures.

6. Don't shield them from natural consequences such as speeding tickets or seat belt fines.
7. Don't lose sleep over minor infractions Remember that adolescents can be annoying without being obstinate or requiring correction.
8. Be patient and forgiving.
9. Treat your teen like your peer when possible. Perhaps you will see a small spurt of maturity.

The last thing that parents want is for our relationship with our adolescent to hit rock bottom. Despite their stubbornness, teens rely on parents to break through their barrier of rebellion. All those defenses can be broken with consistent love, patience, and discipline appropriate to action and age.

Biblical Perspective

One of the most intriguing scriptures in the Bible is found in Proverbs 22:6. It states that "if we train a child in the way he should go; when he is old he will not depart from it." After much questioning and contemplation, I came to the realization that there is a noticeable gap in this verse. We jump from training the child to old age. Perhaps this is because the best training in the world will not produce a child that is perfect from inception until death.

It is important to consider that the laws of love of God are immutable. Unlike false existentialism, where one accepts concepts because of social pressure, the laws of God are infallible. We cannot control fate solely by acts of our will. Thus, the human quest for certainty must be based on God's Word rather than on the dogma of imperfect man.

The instability of confusion introduced into training our youth to follow Christ can arise with our own lack of comfort in the Word. It is not that we live with factious spirits and blatantly straddle a spiritual fence. Nor are we motivated by impulses adverse to the aggregate interests of our children. It is just the rudiments of sin that spoil our religious walk: tempers, gossiping, unkind words, lack of a daily devotional life, and the like. These are exactly the traits that, when demonstrated in our youth, we perceive to be rebellious spirits.

There are two methods by which we can align our humanity with our spirituality. The first is to remove the core of the problem. In this instance, the root is sin. Of course, we can't erase sin, but there is a simple solution. We simply must ask for God's forgiveness and assistance so that with His grace He can cover our shortcomings. The other method involves controlling the effects of the core problem, sin. This practice is, by far, the most difficult because it requires a passion for perfection and an ongoing struggle to attain our personal best. Since latent sin is sown in the nature of man, it can be trodden down only through zeal to follow Christ.

It is important to note that both our stability in God's Word as well as our fallibility will be replicated through our children. Okay, should we throw in the towel now and pray for barrenness? No. We are up to the challenge.

The Bible gives some specific instructions in respect to training our children. For instance, in Ephesians 6:4, we are warned not to provoke them. There is no reason to be inflamed with mutual animosity. This only renders our children with the propensity to act out. Pray that your children will see past the person that you are and perceive the person that you want to be. Secondly, in Colossians 3:21, we are urged not to discourage our youth. They are not going to be perfect. Don't make them always be in your debt by their inability to live up to your expectations. Finally, we are told in Proverbs 3:24 that if we spare the rod, we spoil the child. Our parenting style must include discipline. Children are refined by loving structure but decompensate in a chaotic atmosphere.

The story in the Bible of the prodigal son is most noted for its description of a rebellious youth who left home taking all of his inheritance with him After squandering everything, he returned home to be met by a father waiting with open arms and gifts of gratitude. Granted, this parable is meant to demonstrate God's unchanging love for rebellious mankind. However, it is a perfect lesson of how we as parents should love and accept children who defy their upbringing. The prodigal's father allowed the child to stray and did not chase or cajole him. Instead, he waited for the boy to return apologetically and with humility. At that point, the father was free to demonstrate that his love for the son was unchanging and not merit-based.

Despite a stubborn resistance to change, children rely on parents to break through their barrier of rebellion. Elaborate ego defenses can only be broken with consistent love, patience, and discipline appropriate to action and age. Confidently live life in front of your children with the knowledge that you are doing your best. Expect good things from them. If we are committed to God's ways, our offspring will grow on a solid foundation.

Busyness

Reckoning Day

Today is reckoning day;
Woke early with the first ray,
Busyness a constant friend
Toiled vainly 'til the end.

Blinded eyes and heart so cold,
Oblivious to the bold
Theft of eternal value.
Wasted hours give no cue.

Now deeds face the test of fire,
Char, ignite, and then expire.
Oh, to see beyond the veil
All life's chores would seem so pale.

Change perspective, on Him lean.
Loose your grip on all things seen.
Be prepared to hear God say,
"Come, child, it's reckoning day."

*****

Jordan woke early to have a cup of coffee with her husband before he left for work. She had about an hour before it was time to get the children up and ready for school—perfect opportunity to jump on the treadmill for some uninterrupted exercise. A twenty-minute workout left her feeling exhilarated and ready to face the day. Quickly she showered and then made sandwiches to put in the children's school lunches. My, how that hour slid by! Jordan woke her two boys and hushed them so that they would not disturb their little sister. Of course, it was a useless effort. Little Marie toddled out, and together they all rushed through some breakfast. The children then dressed, combed their hair, half-heartedly brushed their teeth, made sure all their homework was in their book bags, and grabbed their school lunches. Then everyone waited by the front window for the school bus. Little Marie still had to be bathed and dressed, so Jordan proceeded to get her ready for the day. There were several errands to be completed, so Jordan buckled Marie in her car seat and proceeded to go to the bank, post office, and gas station. She then received a call from the school that one of the boys had forgotten their signed permission slip for today's field trip. Quickly Jordan drove across town to sign a new form. At noon, she had a lunch date with mothers from her neighborhood group. Glancing at the clock, Jordan figured that she had about an hour and a half to buy a few groceries for tonight's supper, put them away, and meet her friends. At lunch, she put Marie in the high chair and took a deep breath. Lunch was a little harried, as Marie only half cooperated. Then it was off to the mall to purchase clothes for her boys. Both of them were going to be in a concert at school, which required black dress pants and white shirts. They were outgrowing everything they owned. The task wasn't difficult, just time-consuming. Marie had to be strapped in a stroller to restrain her from wandering. To keep her in good spirits, Jordan made a stop at the pretzel shop. By now, it was two in the afternoon, and Marie needed a nap. Maybe she could sleep in her car seat because Jordan had to pick up her husband's shirts from the cleaners and take some books back to the library. Everything was accomplished by the time the bus dropped off the boys. The boys plopped their book bags on the family room floor and sat down to watch cartoons. Jordan admonished them to keep an eye on their sister while she made a lettuce salad and spaghetti. It wasn't an awesome meal, but it would have to do for now. The boys had baseball practice in an hour. Jordan fed the children, left a note for her husband, loaded everyone up, and left for practice. When they returned home, it was time for baths and homework. By now, her husband was home, so Jordan let him help the boys while she bathed Marie and put her to bed. It sounded like the boys were having a pillow fight with their dad instead of homework, but this was their time with him, and he probably didn't want to be too serious. At any rate, everything was finished in time to get them in bed. Jordan quickly threw some clothes in the washer, did breakfast and supper dishes, and collapsed in a chair. She and her husband read the newspaper, watched the news, and went to bed.

Tomorrow will start a new day, which promises to be just as full as today. This is life.

Busyness

The definition of busyness must include all the processes and ongoing behaviors consistent with the accomplishment of perceived tasks. The internal events that underlie and trigger our behaviors are mental processes. As women, we have a self-imposed standard of achievement to which we aspire. The mental processes that we form help us to organize, prioritize, and motivate ourselves to undertake various activities within our realm of responsibility. Some processes are set in stone, as they are tied to basic survival. We do not have to set goals to satisfy appetitive drives such as eating, drinking, or sleeping. Our task with appetitive drives involves setting limits and time constraints. For instance, we must be responsible for what, when, and how much we choose to eat and drink. We also regulate when and how much sleep we choose to incorporate into our schedules. Other processes are independent of survival and are arbitrarily put on a gradient of worth or value. These are involved in the planning that initiates most of our self-determined behaviors.

As we mentally schedule our time, one of the most potent variables affecting our behavior is the pattern of reinforcement. If there are ten items on our to-do list, we are rewarded with accomplishment as they are completed. It is also true that we escape punishment, as late charges, overdue fines, and tardy reminders are avoided. The strength of our desire to complete tasks is manipulated by the reward of accomplishment and the avoidance of negative consequences.

Thus, daily tasks of life gradually become a part of the monotonic routine.

More complicated, however, is the drive to involve ourselves and our children in a myriad of activities. There appears to be boredom with the mundane and a craving for excitement. Anticipatory pleasure propels us to try new things and to become more diverse. Additionally, in some way, the vicarious excitement that we achieve through our children's activities also becomes a part of our own cycle of activity. As a result, we join clubs, set luncheon dates, and enroll our children in sports, music, educational, and religious tasks. Between home, church, school, and community, we gradually fill empty spaces of time with self-imposed busyness.

So what have we concluded to this point? Beyond the need to fulfill appetitive drives and the hustle and bustle to complete necessary chores, we all design a life for ourselves and our families to keep life interesting. Our lives are very much like a garden with our activities being the plants that we sow. The necessary activities would be equivalent to the edible plants. Sometimes, however, we plant flowers. These plants complement our personalities, revolve around interests, and stave off boredom. We choose activities to build self-esteem, to be responsible, or just for fun. We allow our children to become busy for the purpose of teaching them, to flaunt them, or simply to make their lives more enjoyable. At any rate, between their activities and ours, most of us wish that we could expand the hours in each day.

Obviously, we cannot change the length of a day, so what are some solutions to busyness? Keeping that garden organized is crucial. Attach yourself to a calendar and a day planner. With these in tow, it is possible to view all major events and avoid overcrowding. Crowded plants or activities will shrivel rather than flourish.

Once days and events are organized, it is time to prioritize and establish time constraints. It is vital to make sure that the most important tasks get top billing. However, even important events must be limited by schedule. Be the master of your time rather than allowing busyness to take control. Maintenance is a chore that can be adopted from gardeners. They use hoes to get rid of weeds. Nonessential tasks can be discarded or undertaken only on rare occasions. Save your time for what is important. Then water and fertilize the important plants or tasks. How do we do this? Regulate to stimulate.

A close cousin to maintenance is the process of regulation. A task loses its excitement if it must compete with a host of other activities. You may find that involvement in too many great events causes you to be overloaded. Rather than enriching your life, the extra tasks are reduced to merely time consumers. Learn to limit activity and to say no to others and to yourself.

Remember that every activity in which you enroll your child will become a part of your own schedule. In addition to the time it takes to perform the activity, you must add time for preparation and transportation. For example, a thirty-minute music lesson is designed to require a daily practice time of at least fifteen minutes, five to ten minutes of badgering to prompt the necessary practice, a few minutes to take the instrument out and put it away, occasional trips to buy music and parts for the instrument, weekly transportation, and periodic recitals and concerts. Know when to say "Enough!"

What's wrong with this picture? Jan was the mother of two junior high school children. She worked part-time to make ends meet, taught a sixth-grade Sunday school class, and was a member of the PTA and Band Booster Club. The family lived six miles from school, so transportation was an issue for all after-school activities. Both children played in the band, one played volleyball and softball, the other played intramural basketball. The children were active members in their school and respectively enjoyed French club and JROTC. There were school games, dances, and field trips, which all required transportation. The children were also involved in their youth group at church, which met once a week and provided lots of extra fun activities. Weekends and weeknights were all full. Jan took it in stride but was exhausted all the time.

The picture is actually quite normal. However, Jan's exhaustion indicates that a few changes might be in order. For starters, perhaps this would be a good time for her to take a class rather than teach. Sometimes it is beneficial to relax and soak in a little information rather than having to expend energy in preparation and teaching. As far as the school clubs go, they really do not take up a lot of time, and they allow a parent to keep in touch with what is transpiring in the children's school. What about the children's activities? Reduction and carpooling are two words that I would stick to like glue. It does not make you a bad parent to suggest that your children find the activities that interest them the most and then limit their involvement in multiple pursuits. That is the equivalent to weeding and then watering and fertilizing what is important.

A home should be a refuge. If life is too busy, then we lose contact with those that we love the most and tend to grow apart. Keep family life in focus and design extracurricular activities to complement and enhance a solid, comfortable base of operation. Also, allow time daily for personal devotion as well as reading a Bible story and praying with your children. While at home, they need to be taught that a relationship with God is a paramount part of a busy life and not something reserved for church.

Be the master of your busy life. Set limits, be in control, be a good gardener.

Biblical Perspective

In the Old Testament, God rebuked the Israelite people for leaving the temple in ruins while they went about their own busy lives. Haggai 1:9 says, "You expected much, but see, it turned out to be little. What you brought home, I blew away. Why?" declares the Lord. "Because of my house, which remains a ruin, while each of you is busy with his own house?"

In the New Testament, our body is referred to as a temple of the Holy Spirit, and we are urged to honor God with that body. Running hectically around every day can be expected, for busyness is a necessary part of family life. However, our schedule must be managed to allow space for God.

God obviously will not bless a person who neglects Him because of busyness. To quote from *Living Insight*, in the *NIV Bible*, "Busyness feeds the ego but starves the inner person. It fills a calendar but fractures a family. It cultivates a program but plows under priorities."

Busyness is a generational characteristic of mankind that begs to be managed. Each of us needs to examine our lives to guarantee that God is given His rightful place. Church attendance is only one small part of this commitment. Bible reading and prayer should be among our top priorities. According to Haggai, God will not bless a home where He is ignored. Have you ever felt like you were spinning your wheels and getting nowhere? Perhaps it would behoove you to examine your priority list.

Organizing, prioritizing, maintaining, and regulating are all aspects of management, that, when put into practice, will help a household run more effectively. Look upward and outward. Will what I'm doing matter ten years from now? Does it have eternal value or earthly worth? Boldly take control of your home and your life. You may find that a twenty-four-hour day is long enough! After all, it may be a reckoning day. Who knows?

Divorce

Mud-Caked Feet

It was a choice I made to let the path that joined us
Overgrow with weeds
I built fences; planted hedge
Filled my world with magnanimous obligations;
High priority deeds.
An occasional glance was all that was left
Due to the void, an ever-widening cleft.

Like rain our lives dispersed in tiny rivulets
Of private destiny
And pooled in little stagnant ponds.
Heart rusted, rigid, emotionless; mud-caked feet
Dragged in misery.
Day by day our unfinished relationship grew pale.
Without resistance I allowed it to fail.

An imaginary line once crossed defied the return
To spiritual bliss.
Dreams and aspirations all dashed
My troubled soul resisted groping back to vows and preferred
To remain amiss.
Is there too much bad blood, too much pain
Please help me struggle on and remain sane.

*****

Gretchen caught the first hint of a problem when she did the laundry. A shirt that belonged to her husband, Greg, smelled like women's perfume. Her mind did a rapid replay of the past week. There were no blatant warning signs. Greg had worked a little late a couple of times, but this was not unusual in his line of work. Still, the fragrance played on Gretchen's senses.

The painful truth is that divorce is not usually an amiable agreement that occurs between two consenting adults. Marital discord is common to both parties. Sometimes one spouse initiates the separation process, leaving the other confused and saddened. At other times, both parties neglect the relationship, causing it to fail.

Gretchen strained her mind for clues. Their relationship had been frustrating for two or three years. Greg accused her of being lazy for choosing to be a stay-at-home mother. She retaliated in anger at his insensitivity. Gretchen was hurt that Greg didn't understand how much work she actually did in a day to keep the house running smoothly. But never had it occurred to her that he may be so disappointed in her that he would look elsewhere. She had to confront Greg. Probably there was a good explanation for the perfumed shirt.

Even in a bad marriage, there is an ongoing acceptance of roles. One party gets accustomed to the actions of the other, and day by day, month by month, an unhealthy relationship can be perpetuated out of familiar expectations. True, there may not be harmony, but the marriage continues until someone wakes up and decides to call it quits.

It was bedtime before Gretchen had the nerve to question Greg. For a while, he was defensive, and then he coldly admitted that he had been unfaithful. "Why?" questioned Gretchen. Greg went into a long spiel that included comments about how professional his fellow female employees looked, how they enjoyed talking to him, paid attention to what he liked, and respected his feelings. When he would come home from work, Gretchen was always distracted with supper, the children, homework, lessons, and so forth. He felt like he was on the bottom of her priority list. Hurt, Gretchen retorted that he should have matured a little and taken on some household responsibilities. She even said that he should "put on his big-boy pants!" Greg responded that he was tired because, unlike her, he actually "worked." As an aside, he then added that he was tired of the marriage game and ready to move on. Gretchen was incredulous and in shock. She tried to argue, but words wouldn't come to her mind. So they went to bed in silence with the realization that their marriage was in dire straits. One cared, and one could care less.

Divorce

> Divorce /di-vors'/ n. the legal dissolution of a
> marriage; v. to sever the marital relationship with
> a spouse by a judgment or decree

My! Isn't that a simple definition of such a traumatic event? In reality, the process is devastating, painful, and emotional. Bank accounts are opened and emptied, minds are stretched in all directions, and a lawyer becomes one of your closet associates. Some find that marriage is a venturous task that is so daunting that it cannot remain in reality. Others set intangible goals that are not worthy of achievement and thwart progress toward an acceptable and enjoyable relationship.

Warning Signs

Hear that train in the distance? Soon the warning signals will begin flashing, and the wise will see them. A couple does not travel from bliss to blah overnight. Every marriage has its highs and lows. If the relationship was put on an electronic monitor for visual inspection, one could view swings throughout the process. However, rather than stabilizing over time, a marriage entering problem territory would exhibit frequent arrhythmias. When a couple puts no effort into the process, the electronic time sequence measurement would flatline, and the relationship would die.

With a progression toward failure, compassionate dialogue is replaced by negative communications. "Of course, I don't bad-mouth you to my friends. They don't need to know what a bore you are!" This mixed message is designed to be hurtful. I always remember the warning to stay clear of wounded animals because they are apt to bite or scratch because of their pain. The same adage would hold true for wounded people. For some reason, when injured, there is a tendency for a person to lash out. Sometimes the damage to our psyche occurred in childhood or adolescence. At other times, there is a pattern of bad behavior learned from parents. Perhaps the fault lies in our poor communication skills, our lack of compassion, or poor management of marital responsibility. At other times, a marriage crumbles through no fault of our own.

Self-criticism is a warning sign of a failing marriage. It is common to self-deprecate when living with an uncaring mate. There is the feeling that "if I'm half of the relationship, then it must really be a lousy marriage. No decent man would want me." Personal appearance, emotional stability, and ability to be a suitable sexual partner are all internalized as potential personal weakness. These become difficult hurdles to overcome.

Pulling apart also becomes a common feature of a marriage beginning to decompensate. As this process occurs, it can eventually lead to experimentation. The first step is generally to provide personal space to escape turmoil. After a while, an individual feels the need to validate self-worth. As such, risky relationships or extramarital liaisons develop. Sometimes these begin innocently as friendships and slowly expand beyond the limits of morality.

Precipitants

In addition to warning signs, what types of behaviors initiate bad times? Triggers, in this instance, are actions and words that cause marital discord. Sometimes they are unintentional, but for the most part, they are designed to get a reaction. As a relationship matures, it is easy to realize what will make your partner angry.

Fighting and defensive interactions: "Why would I ever expect you to amount to anything? Just look at your parents!" Every negative comment is met with the silence of a "back-at-you" comment. Personal traits are fair game: intellect, appearance, ability, and potential. I call them head shots or arrows to the heart. At any rate, they are the most lethal forms of attack. Silence and sarcasm are designed to be hurtful. Have you ever been around people who have lost self-esteem? They are miserable, and so is everyone around them. Defensive interaction defeats self-worth and leaves the shells of two coexisting individuals.

Lack of respect: Disrespect is another detrimental aspect in a marriage. Martha, age fifty-five, was very bored with her life. She had poured everything into her children, her husband, and her household for thirty-five years. Her children were now grown and gone. Her husband still worked more than forty hours per week. Martha didn't need to work because they had a sufficient income, a nest egg, and retirement plans. But what was she to do with her time? One day, a friend suggested that Martha accompany her to the gambling boat for the afternoon. Martha found her adrenaline pumping as she wagered and won a little money. That fun afternoon turned into many long days of gambling for Martha. She was not aware that she had fallen into the addiction of gambling until she had spent $60,000 of their nest egg, borrowed $20,000 against family assets, and was running up a tab on credit cards. Martha could not face her husband who was planning to retire in five years. Because of disrespect and disregard for her husband, Martha had destroyed their future. Counseling may assist Martha with her newly found habit, but she and her husband face a future of financial woes.

Intentional harm: Beyond a lack of respect is behavior intended to harm one's mate. Patty called her friend Jo to see if she could come over for the evening. Jo sensed the panic in Patty's voice. She knew without asking that Bill was drinking again. After a few shots, this normally sweet man would turn into an angry ogre. He was abusive toward Patty and had given her bruised arms and a black eye in the past. In the background, Jo could hear Bill bellowing out a command to Patty. Jo was hesitant to get involved but feared for her friend's safety. Tonight Jo offered to pick Patty up if she was willing to go to a shelter for battered women. She was not willing, so the conversation ended at that point. Spousal abuse can lead to a miserable life and sometimes divorce. It is surprising how a relationship can slide this low, but some do. Many times, there are substances involved in the picture such as drugs or alcohol Regardless of the cause, the results are still destructive.

Lack of compassion: more insidious than lack of respect or hurtful words and behavior is ambivalence toward one's partner. No longer is there love or longing for one another. It is as though there is no emotional attachment. The prevalent attitude is "Who cares!" Lack of attentiveness will drive away your spouse and cause him to look elsewhere for affirmation. Exclusivity can be caused by lack of balance. Although the following are positive components of one's life, things such as outings with friends, church activities, clubs, and the like can end up dominating a schedule to the point that the marriage is put last. Another possibility in the category of loss of compassion is laziness. In a marriage, this can drive a wedge between people as each is motivated to fulfill personal needs because of neglect from his/her partner.

Thus, there are multiplicities of precipitants that lead to discontent in a marriage. Each serves to distract from the relationship and could eventually lead to divorce. Divorce is certainly not our goal when we say "I do."

Repair Work

What are some things to do to fix a bad marriage? Don't start with an overinflated sense of resolution without the knowledge that repair always involves old-fashioned grunt work.

Putty those cracks: A couple should try to mend the existing relationship by filling in the cracks with meaningful acts and togetherness. In this category would be a walk in the woods, dinner for two, a love note, flowers, and so forth. Endless acts of kindness could be undertaken to add a meaningful touch. The beauty of this plan is that it may reduce the need to scrap a marriage that over time has lost its meaning.

Work together: Marital partners may try their hand at cooperation. True, cooperation is a given in marriage, but for some, it is like working with two left feet. For them, it may be more comfortable to approach the relationship with competition. As two compete to make the marriage more efficient, they may be surprised to find mutual activities in which they can work together harmoniously.

Frank and Velma could never agree on their finances. Both blamed the other for the lack of money that plagued their marriage. Poverty threatened to be their undoing. In an act of desperation, they came up with a novel idea—they split the incoming money as well as the bills in half. Frank no longer had to answer to Velma, nor did she to him. At the conclusion of every month, they would sit down together to determine who was most successful at maintaining a positive balance of money. The loser had to pay for a night out for the winner. Frank loved having a few friends over to watch sports. Velma, as the loser, had to pay for their "beverages" out of her excess funds. On the other hand, Velma loved to plan a quiet night that involved dinner and dancing. If she could be the most frugal, this date could become a reality at the expense of her husband. Both took to the challenge with gusto. Some months Frank would win and sometimes Velma. Over time, their financial difficulties improved through a combination of competition and cooperation.

New game plan: Sometimes it is necessary to come up with a comprehensive new marital plan that is profitable to both parties. At this point, a couple must throw out their current modus operandi, set new bearing, and proceed. There is help available and a lot of resources if needed. Try to relax and have fun. At times, repair is possible.

Point of No Return

There is a point separating repair and dissolution. At this juncture is potential to do marital and personal examination to determine whether there is cause to seek intervention and salvage a disintegrating marriage or to give up and call it quits. Has a relationship error been committed that is so egregious that it could pose a genuine threat to the foundations of your core? Assuming that this is so, and the marriage is deemed irreparable, then both parties may face the emotional, financial, and legal battles that lie ahead. Property, monetary assets, and children all become crucial to the mix.

Heart trouble: What happens if the marital breach is based on emotion? First of all, there is a lot of pain. Both parties tend to blame the other for the downfall and may try to seek revenge. There can be a noticeable change in mutual friendships as those close to the situation refuse to take sides. There is also an extreme shift in routine as each has to fashion new roles to suit a single lifestyle.

Cold divide: When there is a lack of emotion because of a totally disintegrated marriage, then the separation may be seen as simply a legal battle. Financial arrangements are determined by the courts to settle custodial disputes.

Broken spirits/Empty wallets: Generally, separation involves both emotional stress and legal involvement. It is not unlike a death. There is a lot of grief and mourning with accompanying shame, fear, anger, and disappointment. A multitude of legal decisions must be made. It is not uncommon to have to rework the whole arrangement several times before a workable situation is fashioned.

Out with the old/In with the new: When separation ends in divorce, then what? Well, you can go down with the ship, or you can choose to start swimming. It is now time to start from scratch to build a new life with a new perspective. Choose those parts of yourself that contributed to the breakup of your marriage and discard them. Then redefine yourself and begin rebuilding self-esteem. Focus on the positive, not the negative. Learn to trust yourself and others. You can proceed with a life that works for you and for those whom you love.

Biblical Perspective

We as couples may drag through life with "mud-caked feet," but that should not deter us. Marriages are meant to be holy unto God. The contract is durable and binding. Work through challenges with utmost care and with valiant effort, for the institution of marriage is a special, treasured gift from God.

However, what if our world comes crashing down? Sometimes our best efforts are not enough. Relationships falter, and marriages fail. We find ourselves living beyond the limits of what we can endure.

We are now the parcel in the mail stamped "FRAGILE, HANDLE WITH CARE." Despite how our friends and family respond to us, we have the hardest time forgiving ourselves. It is then time to find strength through God's Word.

In John 8:1–11, we read the story of a woman who was caught in the act of adultery and brought before Jesus for condemnation. As a silent rebuttal to the accusers, Jesus began silently writing on the ground with his finger. Slowly, each accuser left the scene, leaving only Jesus and the woman. He told her that he did not accuse her either and urged her to go and sin no more.

If you are suffering the effects of a marital breakup, this scripture in John should give you comfort. In Christ we find compassion rather than condemnation, forgiveness instead of punishment, and acceptance in place of rejection. There is also an offering of hope for the future. Jesus sent the woman on her way with the instruction to sin no more or not to make the same mistakes again. Allow the compassion of Christ to heal your hurt and His belief in your ability to go forward as a challenge to do your best.

If your phase of life involves dealing with a divorced friend or relative instead of experiencing it yourself, you should accept the challenge to help the hurting. In Galatians 6:1–2, Paul instructs us to carry each other's burdens and, in this way, fulfill the law of Christ. Lend a listening ear and let love be your guide. Remember—nobody is perfect, and there by the grace of God I go.

Divorce as an action is painful. For those of us who planned to live life as a mountaintop experience, we may find ourselves struggling on a plateau of despair. At this point, introspection is vital to a healthy psyche. Try to find yourself by getting in sync with God— His love, His forgiveness, and His guidance. Forgive your spouse, forgive yourself, and find strength through prayer and Bible reading to expand beyond your human limitations. Lean on Christ. His strength can carry us when our own strength wanes.

Anxiety

Volcanic Eruption

Life's magma erupted with a violent burst.
It seemed to stray wildly from ordered to random
As it frantically flowed with reckless abandon.

I could not slow my racing heart or breathing
For I had to keep moving to keep up with me.
Now I'm crashing and flailing in a lava sea.

My mind faintly recalls a normal existence
Before pressing thoughts steered my internal clock
Slowly enclosing me in extrusive igneous rock.

I craved for peace and stillness of mind
When like a whisper I heard, "Peace be still.
Lend your body and mind to my will."

I'm trying, dear God, with all of my might.
Please let your presence by my guiding light.

*****

The diagnosis of kidney failure was devastating for Martha. No particular event led to her gradual decline. During a routine physical, it was discovered that her creatinine level was elevated as were other kidney function labs. The news was shocking to Martha who had no family history of this illness. She looked on the internet for diets that may reverse her condition. It was hard to cut out many of the foods that to that point had been staples in her diet. However, she did her best. The effort was futile, and Martha's kidney function slowly worsened. As it did so, Martha's mental state also took a turn for the worse. Worrying about her future, Martha could not sleep, and through long, sleepless nights, she pondered her fate. She procrastinated going to the nephrologists because of fear of what the next move would be. She had heard horror stories about dialysis. Martha's blood pressure climbed as her anxiety rose. She avoided the fistula surgery, which would prepare her body for dialysis. Martha's name was also put on a kidney transplant list, and she was told to stay close to a phone in case it was necessary for her to make a quick trip to the hospital. Staff in the medical offices was kind to Martha. However, she was not kind to herself. Martha was overwhelmed with anxiety. She finally resolved that dialysis was probably the only thing that would preserve her life. It was at this point that she received a call from the transplant office. A donor kidney had been found, which they believed would be a perfect match for Martha. It was a match, and now she is on antirejection medication to preserve that awesome gift of life. The anxiety and high blood pressure subsided when the crisis was resolved.

Sometimes, however, internal breakdown is not related to an obvious predetermining factor. Sarah successfully balanced a family and a career for several years. Her marriage was on solid footing, finances were not an issue, and her children were absorbed in high school with activities and friends. Sarah could not explain what was wrong, but she could not seem to pull herself out of bed in the mornings. Grooming and picking out clothing were daunting tasks. Then she had to go to work, try to face colleagues, and undertake her assigned jobs. Truth be known, she spent most nights tossing and turning with only fleeting sleep. As Martha's own heart beat rapidly, her husband's steady breathing bothered her. So did the night sounds and the bathroom night-light. Her mind would jump from thought to thought. As she bantered with herself, the topics were disjointed and meaningless. Eventually, the sun would rise, and Martha would undertake the day's routine again. A trip to the doctor verified that the tightness in her chest was not physically triggered. What could

Martha do? For the first time in her life, she was facing full blown anxiety.

Anxiety

The term *anxiety* can refer both to a symptom of some external stressor or an emotional response to subtle internal stimuli. The affective manifestation is similar, and the emotional response can range from short-term to pathological.

The provocation of anxiety may be a real event. As such, it is the duration of the symptoms, which then demonstrate normal response or neurotic behavior. Proportionality of behavior in respect to the event must be accounted for when evaluating whether a response is an initial reaction or an ongoing maladaptive activity. As an example, a person hiding in a basement during a tornado may experience rapid breathing, sweating, accelerated pulse, and crying. This would be considered a normal or expected reaction to a traumatic event. If these symptoms persist for weeks or months after the cessation of the tornado, then this individual could be labeled as suffering from anxiety.

On the other hand, some individuals exhibit symptoms of anxiety without an identifiable trigger. The irrepressible feeling of being unsettled seems to be unexplainable.

Amy was in her sixties and was a successful businesswoman. Her career was satisfying, and life at home was uneventful. However, without explanation, she could no longer sleep through the night. Amy would awaken with a rapid heartbeat and felt as though she could not get enough air. She would either pace the floor or go out for a drive. A trip to her doctor proved that there was no medical explanation for her condition. As the symptoms persisted, Amy finally had to resort to antianxiety medication. She also spoke with a psychologist who helped alleviate her worries.

As it manifests without a trigger, this form of anxiety can be more surreptitious for the individual but is just as real. It can occur as an ongoing mental state or in spurts called panic attacks. Repression of the feeling is ineffective since it originates in the unconscious mind.

However, regardless of whether one's state of anxiety has a trigger or develops from the psyche, there are several therapeutic interventions, which can be effective. Some individuals resort to encouragement from trained personnel such as pastors or counselors. Others require formal psychoanalysis or psychotherapy. Many find that biochemical therapy can be used effectively as medication is utilized to attack the manifested symptoms. Fortunately, there is help available to deal with anxiety.

Thus, anxiety is an issue with which many women must deal. Sometimes we can point to a trigger, and at other times, we cannot. At any rate, there is hope and assistance. Do not suffer silently. With God's help, we can have the calm assurance that we are not alone. The Holy Spirit is referred to as a "Comforter." Ask for God's help to choose the appropriate intervention to deal with your situation. The Bible states, "Peace I leave with you, my peace I give unto you." Open your heart and mind to receive God's gift of peace as you seek appropriate help.

Biblical Perspective

What does the Bible have to say about anxiety? In Matthew 11:28–30, we are urged to go to God if we are weary or heavy-laden. If we do, we are promised rest for our souls.

Sometimes exhaustion stems from a self-imposed lifestyle that is designed to fit too much activity into a twenty-four-hour span of time. Allow God to help you organize, prioritize, and make needed cuts. John 14:27 tells us not to be afraid or let our hearts be troubled because God will give us peace.

What if your anxiety is due to self-recrimination because of poor choices? Perhaps you have allowed immorality to creep into your thoughts or behaviors. Maybe you have made financial errors, which demonstrate devastating lack of judgment. What if you just lack motivation to maintain a healthy weight or lifestyle? You have lost self-confidence and pride. By turning our existence over to God and asking for His help, we can slowly regain control, which leads to peace. Second Thessalonians refers to Jesus as the Lord of peace. He desires that our hearts be calm.

One aspect of finding peace involves a thankful heart. Colossians 3:15 urges us to be thankful and to let the peace of Christ rule in our hearts. One couple with whom I spoke had a troubled marriage because of the wife's ongoing high anxiety level. She had yet to discover that through adversity comes innovation and problem-solving. Their marriage had potential to grow stronger as the husband helped mitigate his wife's fears with support and positive reminders of how thankful he is for her abilities and contribution to their marriage. Thankfulness can assuage anxiety and ease fears.

Why do individuals try to handle every situation alone? Sometimes our shoulders are just not wide enough to carry the load. If the problems are external, ask for help. Friends and family can usually lend support. This does not make you less of a person. If the struggle is internal, seek professional help. Counseling and medication can be of great benefit. Regardless of whether your anxiety is external or internal, ask for guidance from above. Psalm 55:22 tells us to cast our burdens on the Lord so that He can sustain us.

Finally, have you ever considered that there are other women who are suffering just like you? Focusing outward rather than inward has a healing effect. God reserves blessings for those who help the hurting.

Throughout the Scriptures, we can find direction to turn to God when we are anxious and allow Him to calm and reassure us. This does not mean that we should neglect the social, psychological, or medical help that is available. Rather, in conjunction with assistance, we can rely on Jesus to calm and quiet our busy minds and nerves. Jesus wants us to turn to Him, and He has promised to be our ever-present help in times of trouble.

Situational Depression

Ambivalent Feet

Ambivalent feet seem to lead nowhere
As surrounding tasks bid for completion.
A clouded mind rendered useless by care
Finds itself circling as nothing gets done.

Dense, heavy vapor envelops the room
While a mist of tears obscures all escape.
Despair is kin to beckoning doom.
Must try to focus before its too late.

Speak, oh my God, with calm reassurance.
Give strength and resolve to deal with this grief.
Midst turmoil uphold despite my weak stance
And with guiding hand provide sweet relief.

*****

The wedding was beautiful and went off without a hitch. For the past year, Martha and her daughter had carefully planned every last little detail. Now what? Martha sat at the table with a cup of coffee and the newspaper, reading the same article over and over. She just couldn't focus. Her mind told her that she should be elated. Her daughter was now happily married and had a beautiful home across town. Slowly Martha ambled across the room and flipped on the television. She wasn't interested in anything, but somehow the noise was comforting. A tear slid down one cheek and then the other. Martha was too tired to even dab them away. Simultaneously, she was frustrated with herself for being sad and confused as to why she was so upset. Then with panic, Martha realized that she must be a victim of the empty-nest syndrome. She couldn't turn back the clock, so what was she to do? There was no way that her daughter could find out that Martha was sad. It would mar her happy new life. Martha's husband wouldn't have much tolerance for this sentiment either. She had to recover pronto! But how could she do this? Martha sank into a recliner and tried to pull herself together.

Situational Depression

Depression is an insidious disease that creeps upon its victims before they are aware of its presence. It goes beyond sadness in its debilitating effect and duration. In fact, a state of sadness probably will not even be categorized as depression unless it lasts for at least two weeks and is accompanied by a host of other negative symptoms. Some people do not need a precipitating problem to enter an episode of depression. For them, it is generally recurrent and must be addressed by ongoing medication. For most of the population, however, depression is based on a triggering event, which affects the person in a way that recovery is best aided with intervention.

Situational depression can impair ability to function as the mind clouded with grief loses its ability to maintain concentration. Doom and gloom mentality sits at the forefront of one's brain, and worry becomes a constant companion. It seems as though it is necessary to plod through simple tasks at a snail's pace. Lost is the ability to keep up with current surroundings, and the individual feels useless and impaired.

Sometimes depressed people feel that they have caused the triggering event even if that is impossible. This fear can develop into an irrational plaguing feeling of guilt. There is also the embarrassment of an inability to climb above circumstance. It feels to them like people, even friends, would look down on them or look at them as incapable.

Others have a problem communicating because of constant tears. Who wants to talk when it is necessary to choke back tears all the time? It is easier just to climb into a private, silent shell.

Conversely, for some depressed people, tears will not come. It becomes impossible to release emotion because they feel that they are empty on the inside. Their mood is dysthymic with a congruent affect.

Examples of situational depression include postpartum blues, empty-nest syndrome, illness or death of a family member, loneliness of old age, financial ruin, or any other event that brings devastation into your life.

For some people, the situation may be nothing more than seasonal change. As winter approaches with diminished sunlight, there can be hormonal or physical changes in one's body causing a feeling of drowsiness or lack of motivation.

Another common trigger for situational depression can be related to social media. If one confronts a situation in which negative feedback is given, then it can affect self-perception. Tainted self-worth can lead to a downward mental spiral.

Busyness can contribute to situational depression in two ways. First, we may be bombarded with mental congestion, which makes easy decisions difficult and overwhelming. Second, busyness sometimes leads to a necessitated pattern of existence, which requires limiting sleep. Over time, our body and mind are incapable of replenishing energy. Lack of energy can lead to depression as life becomes more and more difficult.

Drastic change in life with no obvious solution is a common depressive trigger.

Kathy knew she did not want to end her life when she took a handful of pills. She rationalized that maybe she could just go to sleep and not wake up for a day. She so desperately needed to escape. Kathy found that tasks were too difficult to accomplish because of a lack of interest or energy. The phone was left unanswered as messages accrued. Social events had lost their appeal, and she just stopped attending them. Even going to familiar places like church or family gatherings had become drudgery. What had happened to Kathy? Her husband had passed away six months ago, leaving her with a mortgage payment, two car payments, and two high school children who ate like horses. She worked full-time but had done that while her husband was living. Now the income was drastically reduced because of the lack of her husband's income. Life insurance had paid for his funeral and some of the astronomic medical bills but left nothing for daily living. Creditors were hounding her to the extent that Kathy refused to look at the mail.

Kathy loved her children with all her heart and did not want to hurt them, but she could no longer cope with sorrow, debt, and responsibility. Her drastic move opened the eyes of her extended family who were only too happy to help. It was also at this time that Kathy realized that she needed to reach out for some professional intervention.

Why do some people who experience a situation in life fall prey to depression, while others remain stable? It is believed that there may be a biological predisposition to experience conflict in various ways. Together and individually, hormones, genes, and neurotransmitters in the brain can function to manipulate thought process. As depression creeps in, individuals crave to isolate and ruminate about negative things. This could include self-deprecating thoughts as they lack the ability to redirect their thinking. As such, they lack the drive to improve their status. This lack of motivation becomes self-fulfilling as they cannot set and achieve goals. A foreboding sense of worthlessness and failure dominates their feelings. Stuck in this rut, it sometimes feels like self-medicating may be a good solution. Individuals can fall prey to alcoholism, drug addiction, or eating disorders when they are compromised by depression.

Deal with depression

1. Realize that you are suffering from depression and try to identify the situation that triggered its onset.
2. Vow to be active rather than passive in your approach to overcome your sadness. Be open with friends and family because isolation is your enemy. Be honest about how you feel, but then be ready to move on.

3. Change your focus from inward to outward. There is no faster cure for depression than finding someone who needs help or attention and then providing the needed assistance.
4. Stay connected to family and friends on a level unrelated to your sadness. Visits and conversations are freeing activities.
5. Utilize professional help. It is not demeaning to talk to a pastor or therapist.
6. Take medication if needed. Your doctor will be the best judge of this.
7. Rather than dissolving in sorrow, give praise and thanks to God. What a magnificent solution for life's hardest moments. In the Bible, it is referred to as a "sacrifice of praise."

As humans we are sure to face situations in life that push us to the limits of our endurance. Turn to God. He has hands extended to be our confidant and friend.

Biblical Perspective

In the Bible, depression seems to be characterized as dismay. Isaiah 41:10 urges us not to be dismayed for God will strengthen, help, and uphold us with His righteous right hand. So even when we feel helpless and hopeless, God is holding on to us. When we feel as though we cannot put one foot in front of the other, God promises in Psalm 40:1–3 to lift us out of the miry bog and put our feet upon a rock. God even promises to put a new song in our mouth, a song of praise to God. Psalm 34:18–19 says that the Lord is near to the brokenhearted and saves the crushed in spirit, and Psalm 3:3 says that He is the lifter of our head. In Matthew 11:28, we are told to come to Christ if we are heavy-laden, and He will give us rest. First Peter 5:7 says to cast all our cares on Christ because He cares for us. Psalm 34:17–18 says that when the righteous cry for help, the Lord hears and delivers them out of all their troubles. The Lord is near to the brokenhearted and saves the crushed in spirit.

The Bible is full of verses relating to depression and broken spirits. Throughout the Scriptures, we read that God wants us to turn to Him. He promises to be there for us just like a parent. Protection, security, and enduring love emanate from our heavenly Father. Yes, we will have struggles because this is life. However, through everything, we can rest assured that God cares. Facing difficulty can be easier with the realization that we are never alone.

Personal Tragedy

The Ogre's Bed

On the verge of annihilation she stood
As life's clock paused briefly with consideration.
Behind her stood silent bliss, beckoning and coy,
Ahead lay her existence void of elation.

As potential freedom and present pain cast stares,
Each vied for strategic position to grab prey.
From their watchful spheres these forces jostled to tear
Her from the precarious point where her mind played.

Empowered with resolve she turned to tread her path.
'Tis a somber pleasure to face one's pain with strength.
Though wearied by life's cares she bore no wrath.
Her landscape now afforded life to reach its length.

*****

Angry waves emanated from the family room as sixteen-year-old Jenny and Sam, her boyfriend, communicated through clenched teeth and hushed whispers. Nicole, Jenny's mother, did a silent high five to herself and breathed a sigh of relief. Jenny and Sam were too intimate for their own good, and Nicole prayed for the day that Jenny would realize this fact. Sam went home early, and Jenny went to her room and disintegrated in tears. Nicole let her cry for a while and then went to Jenny's room to lend motherly support. Jenny retorted with silence. After Jenny spent a week moping and crying, Nicole finally worked up the nerve to talk to her. She simply stated, "Mom, I'm one month pregnant." Nicole was not prepared for these words and felt the room spinning. She had to sit down and feared that she would throw up. Nicole then hugged Jenny, and together they cried. "Don't tell Dad, please," begged Jenny. Nicole knew this request could not be honored. Their conversation led to sleepless nights and shattered hopes. Little by little, the shock wore off, and the family began to experience their new form of normalcy. Nicole even bought a book so she and Jenny could view the baby's growth on a chart. Jenny stayed in school, and life seemed to go on through bouts of morning sickness.

After two more months, Jenny began to require maternity shirts to accommodate her changing figure. This upset her and made going to school more embarrassing. Jenny had been in communication with Sam during this time, which was met with mixed feelings by her parents. Life was so complicated!

Little did Nicole know that the real tragedy had yet to begin. It was about two in the morning when she woke up with a start. For some reason, out of the blue, Nicole felt something was wrong. She went to Jenny's room and woke her. "Is everything going well with your baby? I have a bad feeling." Jenny slowly turned over and retorted, "I had an abortion. I am not ready to be a mother, and Sam doesn't want a kid." Nicole could not respond because the pain was immeasurable. The little girl who could not get a broken arm fixed without parental consent now had made a medical decision that could haunt her the rest of her life. Nicole entered a period of deep depression and closed herself into a shell. She grieved for the grandchild she would never know, for the fractured relationship with her daughter, for a life that had gone terribly awry.

For the first time in her life, Nicole faced a personal tragedy that was larger than life. There was no solution. Love, forgiveness, and time were her only allies. In desperation, she turned to God with the realization that her life had changed forever.

Personal Tragedy

There's an old myth that tells about an ogre whose job was to build beds. He would then capture people to sleep in his creations.

If his captive did not fit the bed, he would cut off part of the body or stretch that person until the body and the bed were equivalent. Ouch!

Of course, this is just a ridiculous myth, but unfortunately, this is exactly a picture of how we deal with tragedy. Each of us has a perception of how we believe that our life should operate. When a complication arises, we rush to adjust it quickly so as not to disturb our perfect image of existence. This is normal and healthy. However, what happens when the problem that arises is so tragic that we cannot cut if off, stretch it, ignore it, make it go away, or fix it? We meet our ogre and a mismatched bed.

Personal crisis is a universally shared development that, at some point, affects every individual. By definition, it involves a calamity or a disastrous event that occurs in one's life. When personal tragedy envelopes us, it has the effect of subordinating all other aspects of life. Existence is mandated to adjust and manage itself as the tragedy takes center stage. Included in the category of catastrophic life events are death of family members, financial ruin, divorce, grave illness, oppositional children, and major events that negatively dominate life at a certain stage.

No matter how we try, it is difficult not to get caught up in circumstances. An egocentric, self-enclosed, and personal outlook is bound to exist as we drown in our disaster. Concurrently, we seek impossible victories and prepare our minds for inevitable defeat. The "I can fix it" mentality is challenged by personal disaster.

As the need to fix a situation grates up against the inability to make things right, one can never achieve satisfaction. Everything we do becomes tainted. Hurting people must eschew the urgent need to control their tragedy, as this now becomes self-destructive. With the overwhelming urge to manage life and ongoing inability to make any headway, we can easily slide into a questioning and finger-pointing mode: What if I had done this or that? Why didn't God answer my prayer? Am I a bad person? Am I crazy?

Pain from personal tragedy causes significant distress. It impairs our ability to function on personal, social, and/or occupational levels. Our ability to effectively deal with the pain plays an important role in the severity of our reaction and our ability to maintain a functional lifestyle. The deficit we experience is not intentionally produced, nor is it feigned.

In the acute phase of a personal tragedy, it is normal to experience shock, anger, sorrow, and a whole range of negative emotions. However, one's life only becomes dysfunctional if the acute symptoms are allowed to become chronic. We must be cognizant of excessive or unreasonable grieving or reactive behavior. Maladaptive behaviors must be dealt with and extinguished. This may be easier said than done.

Megan and John were a young married couple with two small children. They lived a normal middle-class existence. There was work, church, social functions, family, and a happy home. Then one day, when Megan was dressing her children to go to the pool, she noticed an unusual lump on three-year-old Andrew's neck. This was the beginning of eighteen months of doctors' visits, hospitalizations, and grueling chemotherapy. Andrew did not survive. The devastating loss prompted a lot of soul-searching and questions.

The loss of a child drove Megan and John apart, as each was consumed in private grief. John even pointed his finger at Megan and asked why she didn't notice the lump sooner, before the cancer had spread. After all, she was the one who usually dressed and bathed the children. Megan already blamed herself, and the added accusation from John proved to be too much. Time could not be reversed. There was nothing she could do now. Her baby was gone. Megan became consumed with thoughts of ending her anguish. The only thing that prevented her was the love she had for her remaining child, three-year-old Sarah. How could this personal tragedy and others like it be addressed?

1. Time is a healer. Allow passing days to ease shock and give you a clearer perspective.
2. Do not retaliate with negative emotions and words when a spouse or relative reacts to personal tragedy in a negative manner.

3. Ask God for help. He is sovereign and knows the end from the beginning. Try to turn impossible situations over to Him and rest in the assurance that life is in His hands.

4. Ask questions. Step back and assess the situation. Then allow reasoning to free you from guilt.

5. Correct any behaviors that contributed to your tragedy. Give yourself space to change as needed.

6. Do not push others away. Allow their concern to uplift you.

7. Do not be a drain to those around you. If you cannot control your emotions, then find a quiet, personal place to pull yourself together.

8. Find an entertaining activity to force your mind away from your calamity: read, write, run, ride a bike, watch movies, or do anything that requires your entire focus.

9. Find someone to love. Reverse inward focus by doing nice things for others.

10. Be willing to start over if need be. Life is always evolving. Sometimes it is jolted in unexpected directions.

Biblical Perspective

Look up—don't give up! In the Bible can be found many verses that instruct a person in the midst of a tragedy to give the problem to God. Psalm 55:22 tells us to cast our burden on the Lord. It says that He will sustain us and never permit the righteous to be moved. This scripture and others do not promise that God will correct the problem, but rather that He will give us stability and keep us secure through our disaster. If God chooses not to heal me, then He will give me grace to accept the outcome. If I lose everything financially and am forced to live at a lower socioeconomic level, then He will sustain me. If my child chooses to rebel and rejects me as a parent, then I will be given the strength to love myself. The list is big enough to include every problem, and God is big enough to give us the grace to endure whatever comes our way.

Second Corinthians 4:18 says, "For the things which are seen are temporary but the things which are not seen are eternal." We must change our focus. Do not concentrate on the terrible event that has occurred in your life. Instead, focus on eternity and how you must live in respect to eternal values.

Romans 8:18 says, "For I consider that the sufferings of this present time are not worthy to be compared with the glory which shall be revealed in us." Personal tragedy must be weighed in terms of eternal life. God sees the bigger picture. Yes, He cares about our suffering, but at times, He chooses not to remove it. If you do not believe this, just read the story of Job in the Bible. Job suffered extreme personal tragedy as God tested his resolve to remain true to eternal values. Throughout the ordeal, Job chose to bless God and accept his fate. Like Job, we must accept our circumstance, be gracious, and grow closer to God.

In times of personal tragedy, God provides direction, grace, and a promise to be with us and to never forsake us. In turn, our resolve must be to not forsake God. You may feel that you are uniquely targeted with a painful situation. However, everyone experiences a tragedy of one sort or another. Pull yourself up by the bootstraps. Let time be a healer. Allow the love of God, friends, and family to comfort you. Be the master of your own mindset. To be an overcomer is a personal choice. You can do it!

Devastating Illness

Small Umbrella

A storm blew in with all its fury leaving destruction
In its path.
My small umbrella met its match.
Treacherous wind and driving rain; poignant illustrations
Of God's wrath.
Have the Heavens withdrawn sustaining care?
The burden I'm carrying is hard to bear.

To no avail are aspirations, dogma, rhetoric,
And theory.
Conscious efforts all fall short.
Sad, empty, devoid of meaning, I find myself
Fatigued and weary.
Through sleepless nights, questions plague my troubled mind.
Why did you take my health? This is so unkind.

With empty arms and aching heart I inquire of God what
I've done wrong.
His outstretched hand then beckons me.
Slowly I tread the darkened path; my constant companion
For so long.
At last I yield my will to God's sovereign plan
With knowledge that I am secure in His hand.

*****

My husband and I took our young grandson to an ice cream estab-
lishment. The owner of the restaurant had struggled with diabetes

for many years and found it to be a daunting task. In the process, he lost one leg up to his knee and waited on our table with a limp and a cane. Our grandson was incredulous! With wide eyes and seriousness, he asked the man, "Are you a pirate?" With a big grin, the owner assured our grandson that he was indeed a real pirate and then brought him a few pennies as proof of booty he had collected from Captain Hook. What a good sport!

Devastating Illness

There are the trials and the drudgery of enduring ongoing illnesses. We have had friends dealing with Parkinson's disease, multiple sclerosis, diabetes, and arthritis. However, in addition to ongoing illness are devastating diseases that come on suddenly and rock your world. Sickness of a family member or oneself thrusts you into crisis mode. It seems like the inability to stop time's forward march has a traumatic effect. Devastating illness has the potential to cause affective, cognitive, and behavioral malfunctioning. To demonstrate, I will retell a story from a boy's file of writings that related his experience in walking right up to death's door with a family member.

> He was scary…Halloween eerie. From the perspective of a three-year-old, his face seemed to blend up into his head. Hair all gone and face devoid of lashes and brows. The man in my parent's bed was ghostlike, taking your breath away. He couldn't sit up and threw up a lot. He didn't recognize me. No way could this be my father. Strong arms and love of sports; could throw a football or shoot hook shots better than anybody. He didn't even care if he got grass stains on his knees. In a crowd his head stuck up above everyone else. Long feet…He would put one foot in front of the other to show me that two feet could make a yard. Sense of humor that made people laugh, subtle in his manner. Loved baseball games, gave pointers

to keep your eyes on the ball and not to run to a base if someone else was already on it. Smiled when he listened to screechy violin music… my music. Showed him how to play "Twinkle, Twinkle" five different ways. Now I peeked at him lying in the bed, caught my breath, and took another peek. Prayed to God, not a little Sunday school prayer. I talked about Dad, told God that I was scared. Couldn't tell Dad; he wouldn't hear me. Wouldn't tell Mom; she was too sad. Even now the picture in my mind causes my chest to feel tight. Every one of my senses told me that life would never be the same; that somehow my life had ended when my father went to the doctor. My brother was in school. He was eleven and very brave. He didn't gasp when he looked at Dad; didn't even flinch. Maybe those are the nerves that helped him to become a doctor later in life. Anyway, Mom worked at night, so my brother made a bed in my parents' bedroom. He lay on the floor to help when my dad threw up. Grandpa and Grandma were there too, but not in the bedroom. Sometimes I would make a bed on the floor with my brother. I couldn't help, though, because my legs wanted to run. Sometimes I felt mad and wanted to fight, but I didn't know what or whom I would have fought. Mainly, I pretended to be asleep and prayed. My prayer worked! Dad recovered.

It was as adults that these same two brothers, my sons, had to face the impending death of a parent. This time, it was me. It was Christmas Eve, and hectic preparations had been made for the family gathering the next day. When I went to the restroom, I passed a small amount of blood and had a panic moment. I tried to push the matter out of my mind, but lingering fears prompted me to schedule a colonoscopy. The results were abnormal, and a PET scan was ordered. Then I got the phone call. "Are you sitting down? Are you alone, or is your family with you?" The diagnosis was stage 4 colon cancer. I was in shock to say the least because I actually felt quite normal. I could hardly bear to tell my sons. They were, of course, very supportive. However, by this time, my shock had merged into fear and anger. I could not believe that I had to go through this. I was promised no cure but was given two options: palliative care or chemotherapy. Whew! I tried to weigh the situation. If I chose palliative care, then my decline would be inevitable, but I may still feel well enough to play with my grandchildren for a while. On the other hand, che-motherapy may extend my life, but illness might prevent the time I had left to be productive or fun. To say the least, I was not a happy camper. After much prayer and discussions with family, I opted to follow the chemotherapy route. My cancer marker kept going down throughout twelve rounds of chemotherapy as proof that the treat-ment was effective. Subsequent to chemotherapy were surgeries first for liver tumors and then colon tumors. This was followed by a reg-imen of CT scans. I have been declared to be in remission thanks to many prayers and talented doctors. Oh, and those grandchildren continued to be a delight throughout the process.

What can be learned from devastating illness:

1. It has no respect for a person or family.
2. Expect shock that turns to anger and later to resolve.
3. Follow medical advice to the best of your ability.
4. Swallow your pride and allow family and friends to help.
5. Keep a positive outlook and be determined to beat the odds.
6. Find great distractions and stay busy.
7. Maintain the best diet and exercise regimen possible.
8. Realize that this is bigger than yourself and commit to daily devotions.
9. Pray, pray, pray and allow others to pray.
10. All things are possible with God.

Biblical Perspective

When Jesus died on the cross, He provided a cure for both spiritual and physical man. We can be assured that He hears our prayers. The Bible says that God is so caring that He even sees every sparrow that falls to the ground. In addition to the plan of salvation, the Bible is full of examples of healing. Matthew 11:15 says that the blind receive sight and the lame walk, the lepers are cleansed, and the deaf hear, the dead are raised up, and the poor have the gospel preached to them.

I could list a multitude of examples: stories of lepers being cleansed in 2 Kings 5 and Matthew 8; deaf ears being opened, Mark 7; blindness cured, Mark 8; lame being healed, Acts 3; paralysis being cured, Matthew 9; and an issue of blood being stopped, Mark 5. Jesus even raised some people from the dead, John 11, Acts 20, and Matthew 9.

It is my opinion that Jesus is the same yesterday, today, and forever. If He took stripes on Calvary for our healing, and He hears our prayers today, why wouldn't He be willing to heal us if we ask? Granted, we have medical help today that was not available in the days that Jesus was on earth, but when we have done all that medical science has to offer and are still presented with a hopeless scenario, there is no reason not to rely on God for help. If He chooses to extend our life, He has the power to do so. If not, He has the wisdom to give grace to accept the situation and rest in His will.

Psalms 56:3 says that "when I am afraid, I put my trust in you." Isaiah 40:31 states that "those that hope in the Lord will renew their strength. They will soar on wings like eagles; they will run and not grow weary; they will walk and not faint." Isaiah 41:10 says, "Do not fear, for I am with you, do not be dismayed, for I am your God. I will strengthen you and help you. I will uphold you with my righteous right hand." In Jeremiah 30:17, we read that "God will restore your health and heal your wounds." Psalms 30:2 says, "I called to God for help, and He healed me." Psalm 103:2–4 says that "God heals all your diseases."

Realizing that we are not alone to fight devastating illness is paramount. It is vital to utilize prayer and reading of Scriptures as crucial weapons against hopelessness and despair. Surround yourself with those who will agree with you in prayer and support. God will hear and is faithful to honor His Word. He has our lives in His hand.

Senior Years

Window Seat

She sits silently beside the window,
Watching for a passerby to come her way.
Perhaps someone who ventures by will know
That she's alone and look her way today.

Seldom do they notice or think to wave.
Their hurried lives are like hers used to be.
Closed in a shell she tries so hard to save
Thoughts of her past and happy memories.

Her gait is failing, her skin like paper.
Frailty belies the strength she holds within.
Impotence does not cause her to waver,
But loneliness has reared its head again.

It's not too late to tell her that we care.
Calls and visits would mean so very much.
As the mist of solitude fills the air,
We could change her life with personal touch.

Meanwhile:

She sits silently beside the window
Watching for a passerby to come her way.

*****

Janice stepped across the familiar threshold with trepidation. Last month, her grandmother, Anne, had passed away, and now the family was meeting at her house to divide the belongings. It was almost too painful to bear. There was china, silver, jewelry, furniture, pictures, and so forth. After careful thought, Janice chose the one item that reminded her of Grandma Anne. It was the chiming clock on the dresser in the guest bedroom where Janice always slept when she stayed overnight. Sometimes Grandma would let Janice help her set the time and start the clock by winding it. She was told to always move the hands forward—never backward. Together they did this task with utmost care. Janice took this treasure home with her to cherish as a happy memory. At some point, it occurred to her how appropriate this clock was as a memento, for we cannot move the hands of our life backward—only forward. The present moment can never be replayed as time ticks on with a forward march.

Senior Years

Old age is a time of life like no other. For the first time ever, we are faced with the reality that death is around the corner. Truthfully, that may not be the worst dilemma. Can you imagine trying to deal with declining competence and the inability to interact with life independently? For some, there are social or environmental changes that must be made to compensate for declining ability or skill. Sometimes there is the need to adapt to new resources such as therapy, in-home workers, or meal delivery. There may be a need for new devices such as a wheelchair, walker, or hearing aid. When performance in self-care activities is compromised, interaction between ability and environment has to be studied to make alterations. All challenges must be evaluated frequently to ensure the ability to function independently. The list of complications goes on and on. There is not always agreement between the senior and her children as to what is and is not needed to ensure a safe environment.

How can we gauge when the time is right to become a parent to our parent? It is certainly not a comfortable position in which to find oneself. First, we must look for some hints that the life of our loved one is beginning to decompensate. Perhaps there is unexplained weight loss, frequent falls, or unexplained injuries. Sometimes personal hygiene begins to deteriorate as the relative forgets to bathe or wash her hair. Forgetfulness is common as burners are accidentally left on or candles are left burning too long. A little extra supervision may be needed at this point. However, sometimes the deterioration is more extreme. Suspiciousness can become common. Do not be offended if you get accused of hiding the misplaced television remote or the car keys. Hmm, maybe you actually did hide the keys! At times, behavior becomes so bizarre that the parent who always looked as though she stepped out of a catalogue emerges wearing a night gown and flip-flops. By this juncture, there are times when the person is not always oriented to person, place, or time. This might occur sporadically with the occasional loss of one orientation or another. At other times, the onset is gradual and insidious as it eventually claims every orientation.

Liz, a middle-aged lady, is currently dealing with an elderly father, Ben, who is pretty self-sufficient and a mother, Lou, who is suffering from Alzheimer's disease. It is difficult to deal with two aging parents, especially when one is losing ground mentally. Not long ago, Ben and Lou were shopping in a grocery store when Lou decided to take a drive. Why she made this decision and how she happened to have a set of car keys is still a mystery. Once in the car, she called Liz to say she couldn't get the car started. Liz knew her parents had planned to go shopping and hurried to the market. It was too late. Lou was already gone. Ben was in a panic, and Liz decided to drive up and down the streets to try to locate Lou. After about thirty minutes, she returned to the store to tell her father that they had better call in a missing person report. As they were discussing this option, Lou pulled in the parking lot and angrily jumped out of the car, as fast as an eighty-five-year-old lady could jump. She raised her voice at Ben and asked, "Why did you go to the store without telling me? I have looked everywhere for you." Then she looked at Liz and said, "I suppose it was your big idea!" Of course, there was no reasoning with Lou, and the situation had to be dropped. They were just thankful that somehow Lou made it back to the grocery store. By the way, Ben confiscated Lou's set of car keys.

Isn't it fun dealing with old age? In the Bible, there is a "dust to dust" decree. But what if your family member has not returned to dust, but is just getting dusty? I must admit that I have been blessed or cursed with an insatiable compassion for hurting people. In my family, the elderly members have left this earth with intact minds but failing bodies. My first intervention involved taking in my grand-mother. Hospitalized with congestive heart failure, her strength and condition worsened to the point that nursing home care was sug-gested. Her children agreed, and Grandma was placed in a facility. Outward appearances belied the fact that care was inadequate. When I went to visit, Grandma cried and said that she had lost bladder control the night before. The staff member who came to take care of the problem angrily rubbed Grandma's face with the wet panties and warned her to never do that again! I told Grandma that she was coming home with me. Her children agreed, and Grandma arrived at my house. Whew! I had never lifted deadweight before. Even with my husband's help, the chore was daunting. Grandma did not last very long, but she was safe. She passed with her intact humor and amazing love for God and family. Her heart just quit, and Grandma went home. Back strain or not—I would do it again. And I did.

My husband and I were having a birthday party in our home for one of the grandchildren. My mother was present but not feeling too well. She began vomiting, and I feared that she may give the flu to all the grandchildren present. Mom's condition worsened, and I had a "Duh!" moment. This might be worse than the flu. We took Mom to the ER to discover that she had suffered a heart attack. After many days in the hospital, Mom was released. However, she never regained full strength and had frequent falls. Mom lived alone, so I would visit daily and had a grown foster daughter who was willing to stay with Mom at night. Eventually, Mom fell and injured herself to the point that she had to again be hospitalized. Upon her release, I got a hos-pital bed and brought her to my house. She was put on hospice care, so there were visits from a nurse and a CNA. However, Mom lived for seventeen months before she passed away with a failure to thrive diagnosis. She was bedbound during this time. During the seventeen months, there was a big balancing act as I worked a forty-hour week as a third shift crisis intervention specialist, tried to maintain my household, be gracious to Mom's stream of visitors, and keep Mom clean, fed, changed, and entertained. She was fully alert and cognizant to the end. Even in my dreams, I would hear Mom calling my name and struggle to get up to see what she needed. Then I would realize that I had just had a dream. This occurred for several weeks even after she passed away. Was it worth it? Yes. I would do it again because I continue to have an enduring love for my family members.

Don't be ashamed if in-home care is not the route that you choose for your family member. Not everyone has the means or strength to do so. In reality, it is not always appropriate. My friend cared for her husband with Alzheimer's disease for as long as she could. There was the constant strain of being followed like a mother with a toddler. Car keys had to be hidden, bicycles chained, and escape routes guarded. Eventually, the situation deteriorated as her husband would have the temper tantrums of a child and physically lash out. In-home care was no longer a viable option. There are great facilities offering inpatient care.

However, between the choice of caring for the senior in your own home or sending her/him to a nursing home, there are many great options available today. The spectrum includes nurses and housekeepers, who will assist in the actual home of the senior; senior communities where the senior lives in her own home, but all maintenance and exterior work is done by the community staff; assisted-living facilities where self-care is still an option, but meals, entertainment, and supervision is available; and various levels and types of nursing home care. The level of care can be determined by the needs of the senior as well as financial means. Do not feel guilty about your choice. It is an individual, private, and sometimes painful decision. However, with the exception of premature death, we will probably all be faced with this situation in some form or another.

Biblical Perspective

When Jesus died on the cross, He said to one of the disciples, "Behold your mother." To His mother He said, "Woman, behold your son." From then on, that disciple took Mary into his home and cared for her. The Scriptures are filled with admonitions to help the elderly. First Timothy 5:4 says, "If a widow has children or grandchildren, let them first learn to show godliness to their own household and to make some return to their parents, for this is pleasing in the sight of the Lord." In Exodus 20:12, we are told to "honor your father and your mother, that your days may be long in the land that the Lord your God is giving you." In Psalm 71:9, David urges, "Do not cast me off in the time of old age; forsake me not when my strength is spent." Ephesians 6:2 says, "Honor your father and mother." In Leviticus 19:3, we are told that "every one of you shall revere his mother and his father."

There are many practical ways to honor and care for aging parents. When my mom and dad were elderly, my husband trimmed bushes, mowed their yard, and did car repairs. I made frequent visits and phone calls, transported them to doctor's visits, and helped prepare for holiday celebrations. Not that I am elderly, but my sons have already begun to help. When my husband has some backbreaking projects, they are quick to step in and do all the heavy lifting. Even with their busy schedules, they make frequent phone calls and visits. My life is full and complete because of them and their awesome families.

Children and grandchildren are truly God's greatest blessing. Our love for one another is mutual and enduring. I did my best to care for my family, and in true biblical fashion, they care for me.

Facing Death

Wafting Vapor

Life is as a vapor that quickly wafts through the air.
With restlessness it speeds and cavorts,
In an attempt to test its limitations—yet suddenly
Darkness closes in as existence vanishes.

Futility of effort strikes a resounding chord
And reality decries the frailty of life.
We reason, cling to pleasures, build our empires
Yet stride empty-handed into eternity.

Rich and poor, great and small have sought in vain for approbation
And are discomposed to find that the paths of all men merge.
Yesterday is now today and soon to be tomorrow.
Judgment is pending past a single point of departure.

Now life's lingering atonal melody
Echoes notes begging to be resolved.
Dissonant tones modulate with vibrancy
Before fading into obscurity.

Human minds would sag with hopeless despair
But for the opportunity to wedge an anchor into the Solid Rock
And grasp a hand extended past the void
To guide them to a final destiny and life eternal.

*****

There was some commotion in the garage as my son and his friends returned home from playing down at the lake. The dam on the back side of the lake sloped down to a level area with a little creek. Beyond this was a wooded pasture. I was quite prepared for muddy shoes and clothes, but I was not ready for what happened next. The whole crew began hollering for me to come into the garage. Fearing the worst, I rushed out the door. The boisterous crew were bursting with pride as they revealed their treasures. "Cow bones!" they excitedly proclaimed as they showed me a leg bone, a shoulder blade, and a couple of ribs. I cringed and rushed them outside. I was quite sure that they had happened upon the remains of a deer that had been shot. At any rate, they begged me to allow them to save the bones in a garbage bag so that they could keep them for a while instead of taking them back to the woods. Instead, I handed the boys a shovel and urged them to give the poor cow a proper burial.

Facing Death

Dry bones…many times, these relics are the only monument to a vibrant, meaningful life. We are so caught up in living that it becomes a habit, and we are indisposed to think about death. No individual escapes its snare, and everyone is affected. Yet we avoid the subject like a plague instead of actively preparing for the inevitable. My mind fails to grasp the concept of death, and I do not believe that I am alone in this dilemma. Somehow I just can't look in the mirror and picture skeletal bones.

Over time, I have lost four grandparents and two parents to death. It is a pretty solemn thought to realize that I am now a part of the oldest living generation in my family. I really should be concentrating on how to make the most of what is left of my life. However, assessing life is a difficult proposition. I feel like a letter in an envelope. Time and circumstance have opened the flap, exposing my corners. There are a few rips. I have to work my way free to see outside the package. Therein lies the problem, the current nature of the situation. Right now I'm locked in on details, stuck in the envelope, circumambulating and viewing only the small circle in which I am spinning. It's hard to free my pivot foot, escape the envelope, and look at the big picture.

It's not that I fear death. It just doesn't seem to fit into my schedule. I have just checked the calendar for the third time today. There is so much to do, people to see, and places to go. Am I avoiding the thought of death? No, I'm just living life.

Without being morose, I have to add the thought of death to my current train of thought. Why? Because eternity awaits beyond this life. In addition to earthly preparations such as life insurance policies and a will is the need to spiritually be assured that I am in tune with God and His plan for my life. Daily Bible reading and prayer need to be a paramount part of this picture. It's not college where I cram for an exam at the last minute. In this instance, only God knows when I am scheduled to enter His presence. I must be ready.

Death and its finality leave a lasting impact on everyone that it touches. As we lose parents, spouses, children, and friends, we must find a way to cope. We can react in many ways.

1. Under ideal circumstances, there is an opportunity to gain strength from the experience. We can change and grow in a positive manner and survive death by becoming stronger and more compassionate. This is often observed in families that develop a benevolent foundation in the name of the family member so that others can benefit from contributions. In this way, they keep the memory of their loved one alive.

2. Some people dissolve in total grief over the death of their loved one. As a teenager, I remember my grandmother loudly wailing by the casket of my grandfather during his visitation. The sight and sound were unnerving. Grandma overcame her grief and eventually functioned appropriately. However, the memory of that visitation is haunting.

3. For some people, it is easier to survive the experience by blocking the harmful effect from awareness. Unfortunately, memories then return to bother them for many years. People in this category often manifest guilt over events and

have unanswered questions: Should I have tried to consult a different doctor? Did I tell my family member how much I cared? What could I have done differently?

4. Finally, there are those who break down psychologically and demonstrate that they are incapable of going any further with their own lives.

Forty-two-year-old Sue spent every day drinking away her sorrow. Years ago, as a young, unwed high school girl, Sue gave birth to a premature baby with enduring physical problems that would require full-time care. For the next twenty-five years, Sue devoted her time to rearing and caring for her daughter. Lynn survived beyond her life expectancy as a result of Sue's hard work. Then recently, Lynn needed some minor surgery. Because of complications, she unexpectedly died while in the recovery room. Sue was devastated and could see no purpose to continue her life, so she drank to pass out every day. Words were inadequate. Eventually, with passing time and encouragement from family and friends, Sue can gradually heal, but intervention may be a necessary component of her healing process.

One of my children once said that he wished life was more like a video game. There you can't die permanently because with a couple of moves, you are reborn and can start back where you left off. But that is not feasible. Reality is that each of us has a preset appointment with death. With that in mind, what is my responsibility to ease the pain of my own demise for those I love? Whether my death comes quickly or in small stuttering steps, I should present the picture that I am on solid footing. As a Christian, I am aware that death is merely a passage from life on earth to life with Christ.

I choose to be identified by my life rather than by my death. I am determined to enjoy the ride because life is short, and death is certain. Oh, I will die someday, but not yet!

Biblical Perspective

Just how do women in the Bible deal with death? It seems appropriate to examine the first couple chapters of Luke. He describes a young girl who must have been amazed by the announcement from an angel that she was going to immaculately conceive a son. This was followed by an angelic birth celebration and visits by shepherds, wise men, and her cousin Elizabeth. Surely, all of these events sealed in her mind the fact that she actually was raising the Son of God. Until He reached adulthood, the only unusual thing we read about Jesus is that at the age of twelve, He was found in the temple sharing God's word with the priests. But Mary knew that her son was different from other boys. It was she that urged Him to do something at the wedding in Cana when the hosts ran out of wine. This was the start of Jesus's public ministry. Mary heard His sermons for three years but, like everyone else, was unable to grasp God's divine plan. Finally, on that dreadful day of Christ's crucifixion, we find Mary at the foot of the cross. If it wasn't bad enough to lose a child, can you imagine what it must have been to watch His torture and crucifixion? Mary had no idea that Her son was going to rise from the dead because she was among the women who took spices to the tomb three days later. There are no scriptures that indicate that Mary was angry or bitter or felt deceived. She had been assured that this was God's Son and the future king. But rather than dissolving in grief, she simply waited for the appointed time to put spices on her son's grave clothes.

The Transformation

It was a kiss that chilled the night
And hastened God's plan along.
Arrest at dawn. What cruelty
For a man who'd done no wrong.

With hateful jeers they bore you off.
I trailed close behind.
It hurt me so to hear them scoff
And see torture so unkind.

Your tranquil mood exuded hope,
Though your heart felt agony.

A door opened beyond my scope
When you died upon the tree.

In history a page was turned
And my son became my Lord.

"The Transformation" seems like an unusual title for a poem involving death. In fact, it almost seems like a trivialization of intense grief. Yet no word could be more appropriate. We are all transformed with our last breath. The Bible says that to be absent from the body is to be present with the Lord. The death and resurrection of Christ afforded each of us the opportunity to accept God's plan and allowed us to have the opportunity to spend eternity in heaven. It is this gift that makes death bearable. Paul says that we do not grieve as those who have no hope. We can hold to God's promise that our loved ones who have passed away are safe and secure.

In the book of John, we read the story of two sisters, Mary and Martha, who had to face the death of their brother, Lazarus. When their brother became gravely ill, Mary and Martha sent for Jesus in hopes that He would perform a miracle and heal their brother. Jesus intentionally waited until Lazarus died before He went to Bethany where they lived. He did this in order that His glory might be revealed by the resurrection of Lazarus. Jesus found Mary and Martha in mourning when He arrived. Despite their great sorrow, the sisters responded to Jesus with utmost respect. Martha affirmed, "I believe that you are the Christ, the Son of God, who is come into the world." When Mary saw Him she fell at his feet and said, "Lord, if you had been here, my brother would not have died."

After meeting with Mary and Martha, there is a very unusual scripture. It simply states, "Jesus wept." Why would Jesus cry? He already knew that He was going to raise Lazarus from the dead. I believe that the tears were sorrow for mankind. Death was the result of sin. The generational weight of the sorrow of mankind grieving over the loss of their loved ones overwhelmed the loving Christ at that moment. He wept for mankind. Then He raised Lazarus from the dead as a sign to everyone that He had power over death and the grave.

Another famous mother who lost her son to death was Eve. In Genesis 4, we see that through her own disobedience, Eve ushered sin and death into the world. First, it cost her a happy existence, and within time, it cost the life of her son, Abel. He was murdered by his brother, Cain. No mention is made of Eve's reaction or realization that she was ultimately responsible for one son's death and the other's banishment. She continued successfully as a mother to a third son, Seth. He was chosen to head the genealogical line that continued on throughout biblical record.

What lessons can be learned from Mary, the mother of Christ, Mary and Martha, and Eve, the mother of mankind? It seems that reliance and trust are the key words. If we understand that our families are a gift from God and He holds the power of life and death in His hands, then we must accept that what happens to them and to us is a part of His plan. Comfort can be found in relying on someone bigger than us, especially if we view this being to be omniscient and kind. He will never allow us to experience grief so intense that we are unable to bear the load. God's power transcends death, and He is indeed the author and finisher of life.

We must remind ourselves that we are not alone, nor are we uniquely targeted for pain. From the beginning of time, our trial of death has been replicated in immeasurable fashion. This burden will not be removed from us, but the load can become bearable through faith that our life and the lives of those we love are in God's hands.

In Hebrews 9, we see that God's perspective is timeless and based on eternity. It is amazing to note that He does not measure time by our birth, but rather by our death. First comes death and then the judgment and eternal life. To God, death is simply a portal into eternity. In fact, He refers to our lives only as a vapor and as a preparation for death. As humans, we do not have God's perspective. As such, we feel sorrow for ourselves and for our loss rather than rejoicing at our loved one's going home or looking with anticipation to our own passing. To God, it is simply a transformation.

Through reliance and trust in God's sovereignty and by aligning our perspective to God's, we can face whatever comes our way. Dry bones exist as a monument to life on earth. They are a reminder that earthly bodies are within the reach of destruction. The sufficiency of Christ carries us through this life. The pursuit of infallible perpetuity frustrates mortality as the cravings for this life give way to heavenly rewards.

Notes

Quote in "My Errant Child" from Abraham Maslow's *The Psychology of Science* (New York: Harper and Row, 1996), 15.

About the Author

From a woman to women: After getting a degree in psychology, Patricia Schmidgall has worked for many years as a mobile crisis clinician. Her responsibilities include responding to situations in the community, hospitals, and jails. Depression, anxiety, hopelessness, and suicidal attempts are not uncommon occurrences. Working with shattered people has given Patricia the drive to write about ways to face life's situations. Some are positive and exciting. Others are exhausting. From the perspective of a wife and mother, she has chosen to target women in order that together we can examine God's solutions to every aspect of our lives.

www.ingramcontent.com/pod-product-compliance
Lightning Source LLC
Chambersburg PA
CBHW051224160726
47994CB00002B/740